Singapore

Front cover: The Singapore skyline
Right: Marina Bay Sands

TOP 10 ATTRACTIONS

Chinatown. From food to antiques, this is the place for all things Chinese; don't miss its night market. See page 42.

Esplanade – Theatres on the Bay. One of the city's most iconic buildings. See page 30.

Raffles Hotel. Visit Asia's most famous hotel and have a Singapore Sling at the Long Bar. See page 41.

Orchard Road. With more malls than you can shake a stick at, this is the ultimate shopping paradise. See page 59.

Clarke Quay and Boat Quay. Here you'll find some of the hottest restaurants and clubs in town. See page 33.

Gardens by the Bay. This spectacular green space just minutes from the city is home to thousands of rare plants. See page 31.

Night Safari. The best after-dark activity. See page 71.

Sentosa Island. Touristy it may be, but Sentosa has some of Singapore's best beaches, attractions and historical sights. See page 73.

Little India. Get pleasantly lost in its colourful backstreets. See page 51.

The National Museum. There's more than just history on offer here – check out its handsome interiors too. See page 38.

A PERFECT DAY

9.00am Breakfast

Kick off the day with a typical Singaporean breakfast of freshly brewed coffee with kaya toast and soft-boiled eggs at Killiney Kopitiam, an old world coffeeshop established since 1919.

2.00pm Retail therapy

Across the road from Chijmes is Raffles City Mall where you can enjoy a shopping spree. Or go underground to the CityLink Mall which will lead you to Suntec City's Fountain of Wealth, the world's biggest fountain. The massive shopping mall here has excellent retail outlets.

12 noon Lunch

Try Peranakan fare next door at True Blue Cuisine (47/49 Armenian Street), or Cantonese dim sum at Lei Garden at Chijmes in the City Hall district.

3.30pm Sky high

Take a 30-minute observation ride on the Singapore Flyer, the world's largest observation wheel, which affords a bird's-eye view of the city. After the ride, take a breather at the street food stalls below and munch on some local snacks and desserts.

10.00am Cultural lesson

Take a quick taxi ride to the Peranakan Museum on Armenian Street and learn about the Straits Chinese culture and heritage unique to this part of the world. There are 10 permanent galleries.

IN SINGAPORE

6.00pm River views

For a different view of Singapore, take a leisurely bumboat ride along the Singapore River, starting from the Merlion Park, across the waters from Marina Bay Sands. The pleasant 30-minute cruise on an environmentally friendly electric bumboat brings you to Boat Quay and Clarke Quay.

8.00pm Dinner

Dinner at Marina Bay Sands is a must when visiting Singapore. Walk over to The Shoppes at Marina Bay Sands and choose either French bistro fare at DB Bistro Moderne by Daniel Boulud or hearty Italian cuisine at Mozza Osteria by Mario Batali.

4.30pm Museum time

Meander across the double helix bridge to the lotus-shaped building next to Marina Bay Sands. This is the Art Science Museum which features fascinating art, science, media, technology, design and architecture exhibits.

7.00pm Sunset drinks

Back at the Merlion Park, walk over to Catalunya at the Fullerton Pavilion, Collyer Quay, for pre-dinner cocktails. Soak in the 360-degree views of the city and the glittering marina.

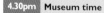

CONTENTS

Features

INTRODUCTION

Singapore is a very small island nation with very large attractions and achievements. Strategically situated on the tip of the Malaysian peninsula between the Indian Ocean and the South China Sea, Singapore has made itself the busiest port in the world, the second-largest oil refiner on the planet and a major international financial centre. While Singapore's astonishing wealth sets it apart from most tiny islands, it is its population that makes it unique. A melding of Chinese, Malay and Indian peoples, this Southeast Asian crossroads has become a model of ethnic and religious tolerance. While the different ethnic groups continue to celebrate their own cultural heritage, it is not uncommon to see the comfortable intermingling of races. A Malay wedding, for instance, can take place right next to a Chinese funeral at a void deck, which is the ground floor of a public housing apartment block. Take a walk around the city, and it's not unusual to see a Buddhist temple, a Hindu shrine and a mosque within two blocks of one another. With policies, laws and practices in place, as well as an innate tolerance and respect among the people of one another's faith and culture, Singapore is sometimes touted as one of the most racially harmonious countries in the world. It also stands out as the cleanest, most efficient and most highly organised society in Asia.

Yet what attracts travellers is not Singapore's wealth nor its social wisdom; it is the shopping, the eating and the ethnic neighbourhoods. Shopping and eating are Singaporeans' main activities and it isn't long before visitors are swept up in these tides of delightful consumerism. Because of its special location and status as a free-trade zone, Singapore boasts good

Aerial view of Chinatown and business district

shopping for clothing, crafts, jewellery and goods manufactured in nearby Malaysia, Thailand and other handicraft centres of Southeast Asia. Again, because of its location, Singapore offers the most diverse culinary experience of any Asian nation. Here, the very best Chinese, Indian, Malay and an array of other international dishes are available, usually at affordable prices.

Finally, for the sightseer and cultural explorer, Singapore offers historic districts to explore, from Arab Street and Little India to the Civic District and Chinatown. There are world-class modern attractions as well, from gardens with conservatories to the world's finest zoos. These treasures are tiny but brilliant isles in an urban sea of modern shopping centres (including one with the world's largest fountain), government housing apartment blocks (home to millions of residents) and skyscrapers (where the money is counted).

It is curious how so much (culturally, ethnically and economically) is contained in so small a space. The main island of Singapore, together with over 63 surrounding islets, covers

Singapore facts

The Port of Singapore is the world's busiest port.

Singapore supports more plant species than all of North America.

Singaporeans' most popular leisure activities are eating and shopping.

The best maths students in the world attend Singapore schools.

The Singapore Sling is still served at the place it was invented almost a century ago, the Long Bar at the Raffles Hotel.

Most Singaporeans (about 85 percent) live in high-rise apartments built by the government.

The Suntec City mall contains the world's largest fountain.

The lowest temperature ever recorded was 19.4°C (66.9°F).

Over 90 percent of Singaporeans own mobile phones.

The number of yearly visitors is more than twice the total population.

Tree Top Walk in MacRitchie

about 699 sq km (270 sq miles) – four times smaller than Luxembourg or Rhode Island, the smallest state in the United States. Yet about half of this land consists of forest reserves, marshes and other green areas.

Green spaces

Singapore's green zones surprise many first-time visitors, at least those expecting to find a colossal air-conditioned city-state of glass and steel housed under a plastic bubble. While crowded and expanding, with a population of 5.4 million (2013), Singapore is not the sprawling patchwork of overlapping suburbs and housing developments one encounters in such large modern cities as Los Angeles. Instead, Singapore can be said to be a vertical Los Angeles. About 85 percent of its residents live in housing estates that consist of neatly kept apartment towers stretching to the sky. These residential towers are distributed across the main island in suburban towns,

Chingay street parade entertainers

many of which have their own subway stations, shopping malls, libraries, community centres and other urban services. Within the tower clusters and between the towns, there are extensive green zones and areas of parkland.

Although linked to Malaysia by geography and by history, Singapore is an independent country, with a population dominated by Chinese (74.2 percent). Malays make up 13.3 percent of Singapore's citizens, Indians 9.1 percent, with the remaining less than one percent comprising Eurasians, Arabs, Jews and other minority groups. There are four official languages (English, Malay, Mandarin Chinese and Tamil), with English designated as the language of administration and Malay as the national language. On the ground, many Singaporeans also speak Singlish, a colloquial language that involves a mix of English, Chinese dialects and Malay. Most Chinese speak a variety of languages, such Hokkien, Teochew and Cantonese, reflecting the various origins of Singaporean Chinese.

One ethnic group that has played a large part in shaping the customs, architecture and cuisine of Singapore are the Straits Chinese or Peranakan, a hybrid race that evolved from intermarriage between Chinese migrants from mainland China and native Malays. The men are known as *baba* and the women *nyonya*, and they have a culture that is a charming blend of Malay, Chinese and British elements. The British themselves also exerted a lasting influence on the language, customs and administration, since they literally created modern Singapore in 1819 and guided its destiny until a new self-governing constitution was approved in 1959.

Wired for success

Singapore is a well-wired nation, with many homes linked to a countrywide network of fibre-optic cables supplying a range of services, from cable TV (more than 100 channels) to broadband internet. The government's goal is to establish an ultra-high-speed, open and seamless network under a masterplan known as iN2015, or Intelligent Nation 2015.

Singapore's transportation system is a showcase of national industry. The subway (MRT) serves more than 2.7 million people daily and continues to expand to all corners of the main island. Over 25,000 taxis serve the city. Cabs are inexpensive, clean and accept a variety of credit cards. Only about a third of Singapore's residents (who enjoy the second-highest per capita income in Asia) can afford a personal car due to the deliberate imposition of high taxes, restrictions on car use and tariffs levied on automobile ownership. This has kept the downtown area

Free Wi-Fi

Free wireless internet access is available at many public places in Singapore under the Wireless@SG scheme. Simply register online with a service provider and using a Wi-Fi-capable mobile device, you can surf away. See page 132.

from experiencing the gridlock and road rage common to other metropolitan areas. Singapore's airport, often hailed as the best in the world, enjoys the same unrestricted flow; clearing customs and immigration is often a matter of how fast you can walk.

Of course, Singapore's efficiency, orderliness, cleanliness and general good behaviour has come at what some critics consider a steep price. Even locals joke that Singapore is a 'fine' country, seeing as how the government has imposed a fine on nearly every objectionable behaviour, from not flushing public toilets to selling chewing gum. Singapore is also known as a country with severe penalties for more serious offences. Caning is prescribed for some crimes; the death penalty is always enforced for drug smuggling. But what some Westerners perceive as an authoritarian city-state, with draconian laws and little personal freedom, is regarded by many Singaporeans as merely the common-sense way to run society. Singapore's economic success and its ability to combat such social ills as drug use, corruption and pollution have made it the envy of many emerging nations and a model for Asia in general.

Respecting elders

In Singapore respect is shown to one's elders; children are obliged to support their parents during retirement years. Under the Maintenance of Parents Act, any parent over the age of 60 who is unable to maintain himself can apply for an order that ensures one or more of his children pay him an allowance.

For sceptical Westerners, seeing Singapore for themselves can be an eye-opener. This is certainly not an oppressed population. On the contrary, Singaporeans tend to be outgoing and cheerful, if a little competitive and aggressive. Some say that social engineering in Singapore has proved a success because it is built on the traditional Confucian and Asian values of the region. While Singapore is cosmopolitan and Western in outlook, it is at the core a society of people who place a high value on family and nation, racial tolerance and consensus.

While a few visitors might judge the politics of Singapore as oppressive, everyone could be forgiven for finding the weather so. Just 136 km (85 miles) north of the equator, Singapore is hot and humid all year round. It hardly cools off at night by more than a few degrees. The lowest temperature ever recorded in Singapore was a 'chilly' 19.4°C (66.9°F). The high humidity leaves most

Economic success continues

visitors drenched in sweat shortly after hitting the streets. Fortunately, ever ingenious Singapore has taken on the forces of the climate, too. In public areas, everything that can be air-conditioned usually is, from buses to shopping malls.

Instant Asia

For some, Singapore is a welcome stopover, its top-rated airport making it the perfect gateway to Thailand, Indonesia, Malaysia, Cambodia and Vietnam. For others, Singapore, with its legendary cleanliness, its widespread use of English and its celebrated sights, shops and ethnic eateries, is a significant destination in its own right – an ideal introduction, in fact, to all of Asia.

A BRIEF HISTORY

With its location at the crossroads of Southeast Asia's sea lanes, it's no surprise that Singapore has long functioned as a major trading post. Malay, Indian and Chinese merchants plied the Straits of Malacca for centuries; Chinese sailors apparently named the island Pu-luo-chung (Island at Land's End) as early as the 3rd century ad. Malays settled on the island by the 7th century, naming it Temasek (Sea Town), and Marco Polo may have sailed by it in the late 13th century. Around the 14th century, the Sumatran prince

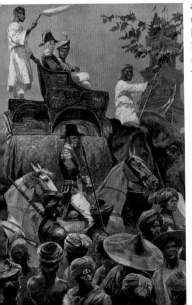

Raffles arrived in 1819

Sang Nila Utama, seeking shelter on the island from a storm, gave it its modern name after sighting what he thought was a lion. More likely he saw a tiger, native to Singapore and Malaysia. The name 'Singapura' is Sanskrit for 'Lion City', and Singapore has been the Lion City ever since, regardless of the fact that no wild lions ever roamed here.

Pirates used the island as a base for centuries, and control of Singapore, the Malay peninsula and the Straits of Malacca wavered between Siamese and East Javan conquerors until the arrival of Raffles, the founder of modern Singapore.

Raffles rules

Sir Thomas Stamford Raffles (1781–1826) only visited Singapore briefly over a four-year period, but he left a giant's imprint on the island. An officer of the British East India Company and a colonial entrepreneur of extraordinary vision, Raffles spoke the Malay language and knew its customs. He governed Java and wrote a history of the region, but his goal was to establish a trading post in strategic waters between Indonesia and Malaysia, where the Dutch, as well as the British, had considerable colonial holdings. Raffles succeeded in this aim when he landed on the banks of the Singapore River on 29 January 1819 and signed treaties with contending Malay sultans, thus establishing Singapore as a British trading post. The Dutch recognised the claim in 1824. In 1826, Malacca, Penang and Singapore effectively became British trading colonies under the British Straits Settlements.

Upon his arrival in 1819, Raffles found an island shrouded in dense jungle and swamp, occupied by a few Malay families and some Chinese traders. Free-trade policies and firm but liberal colonial rule under Raffles' direction soon created a boomtown of 10,000 residents, where 2,000 ships called annually. The sultans sold Singapore's rights to the British in 1824 and Raffles continued his social reforms (abolishing slavery), cleared the land and oversaw an ambitious construction campaign. He opened Singapore to immigration, bringing in labourers, merchants and businessmen from all over Southeast Asia and most notably from China. Raffles, in short, laid the groundwork for the vibrant free port of Singapore that remains in place today.

Raffles created colonial Singapore in astonishingly short order. On his first visit in 1819 he stayed only one week, placing Colonel William Farquhar in command. He returned the same year for three weeks, devising the familiar outlines of the

Singapore in 1870 – junks with Fort Canning Hill behind

city, with its Colonial District on the Singapore River. When Raffles next visited three years later, he relieved Farquhar of command and oversaw the final details of Singapore's reconstruction. By the time Raffles left Singapore for the last time, in June 1823, he had laid the cornerstone for a college that united Malay and European students in East–West studies. The following year, a ship fire destroyed all his writings about the region and his extensive natural history specimens. He died without an heir in London in 1826, a day short of his 45th birthday.

Rubber and tin

The British success in Singapore depended on many elements, including cooperation with the Chinese clan organisations (the *kongsi*) and complicity in the opium trade, which was a major source of revenue from the 1830s onwards. Singapore became a British colony officially in 1867, just before the opening of the Suez Canal in 1869, which further spurred trade in the Straits of Malacca. In the first 50 years after Raffles' appearance, the island's population mushroomed from a few hundred to over 100,000. As the 20th century loomed, the export of rubber and tin became Singapore's major industry. The pirate coves and tiger dens of earlier times were erased; rubber plantations and tin mines ruled the region.

Generations of Chinese migrants from China, many of whom married locals, came to be ardent supporters of British ways. These Straits Chinese dominated local politics and formed the wealthier ranks of the mercantile class under colonial rule, but they kept in touch with the Chinese mainland as well. Sun Yat Sen arrived in Singapore to set up a branch of his revolutionary party in 1906.

The Great Depression in the West swept through Singapore in 1929, hurling many miners and rubber tappers into extreme poverty, but the 1920s also saw the ascent of Singapore millionaires, including Aw Boon Haw, the purveyor of the Tiger Balm ointment. Discontent with colonial rule increased in the 1930s, alongside the rise of India's independence movement and China's Communist Party. The revolution was, however, put on hold by World War II.

The fall of Singapore

Winston Churchill would call the fall of Singapore to the Japanese in 1942 'the worst disaster and the largest capitulation' in English history. The British, confident of an attack from the sea, had

Street hawkers, 1924

built a strong naval defence in Singapore and armed Sentosa Island to the south with large guns, but the Japanese came overland, sweeping down the Malay peninsula on foot and by bicycle, eventually seizing nearby Johor Bahru. Outnumbered three to one, the Japanese nevertheless struck quickly after landing in Singapore, occupying Bukit Timah, which held the British food and fuel depots, and bluffed the British into surrender in seven days. Nearly 30,000 prisoners of war were incarcerated in Changi Prison, near the present airport. They were later led on a forced march through Malaysia all the way to Thailand, where many died building the railway and bridge over the River Kwai.

Residents of Singapore, especially those of Chinese ancestry, were punished more severely than the Australian, Indian and British soldiers, since they had opposed Japan's earlier occupation of China. By the time of Japan's surrender in 1945, about

General Percival led the surrender of British troops in 1942

100,000 Singapore residents had died by execution or of starvation.

The British resumed control after World War II, but their authority was now much diminished and Singapore's desire for political autonomy was strong. The British slowly relaxed their control in the region, creating a Federation of Malaya and also making Singapore – which was predominately Chinese – a separate Crown Colony in 1955. The colony's first chief minister, David Marshall, demanded independence, but Britain would not agree. In the meantime, a new party was rising in Singapore, headed by a new leader who would shape a modern Singapore as profoundly as Raffles had shaped the colonial city-state.

Singapore story

For an insight into Singapore's meteoric rise, read *The Singapore Story*, the vivid and fascinating memoirs of Singapore's first prime minister Lee Kuan Yew, who has deservedly been credited with bringing the country to where it is today.

Lee Kuan Yew in charge

Singapore's modern-day Raffles was Lee Kuan Yew. Lee, born in 1923 to Straits Chinese parents, graduated from the University of Cambridge with honours. Returning to Singapore in 1950, he cast his lot with those advocating the overthrow of the British, helping to form the People's Action Party (pap) in 1955. Supporting labour unions, working with local communists and calling for a merger with the rest of Malaya, the pap won the first internal self-government elections of 1959 and Lee became Singapore's prime minister. Then, quickly cutting his links with the communist and leftist elements, Lee concentrated on severing ties with Britain by uniting with Malaya, Sabah and Sarawak to create the Federation of Malaysia in 1963.

Lee Kuan Yew in 1967

It was not long, however, before Singapore was being viewed as a threat to the new Malaysian republic. Muslim forces hastened the expulsion of Singapore, which came in 1965, dashing Lee's dream of Malaysian unity after just 23 months, but leading directly to Singapore's full independence.

Many doubted whether Singapore had the resources, the will and the genius to survive as a tiny independent nation, but Lee seemed to supply all three elements. As prime minister from 1959 to 1990, Lee has been hailed, especially in Singapore itself, as the singular architect of his nation. He harmonised the contending ethnic forces, brought strict order to society, emphasised efficiency, embraced Western ideas, dealt harshly with his political opponents, ruled the nation like a father and focused unrelentingly on economic progress. So far, his People's Action Party has not spent a single day out of office since independence, and most Singaporeans venerate Lee Kuan Yew as the country's founding father.

The New Singapore

Under Lee Kuan Yew and his successors, Goh Chok Tong and Lee Hsien Loong, Singapore has continued to be one of Southeast Asia's brightest stars over the last three decades. The government's paternal approach has defused racial and labour disputes, public housing schemes have provided most citizens with their own homes, and trade and business policies have attracted plenty of foreign trade and investment. While

Singapore's massive modernisation has its critics and much of old Singapore has been razed, the standard of living has risen to the highest international benchmarks. Social engineering projects – which include banning smoking in public places, outlawing the sale of chewing gum, monitoring public toilets for flushing, imposing huge taxes on car ownership and running state-sponsored matchmaking services – have drawn sneers from overseas, but Singapore is the most mannerly and cleanest of all Asian cities.

From the perspective of Western democracies, Singapore's great achievements have come at the expense of personal and political freedom. Dissidents have been jailed or exiled, and critical publications have been banned (*Asian Wall Street Journal*, 1985) or sued (*International Herald Tribune*, 1994) for unflattering coverage. The local media, from TV to newspapers, have often censored themselves into blandness. The case of David Marshall (1908–1995), one of Singapore's founding fathers, is illustrative. A Singapore-born Jew whose parents

It pays to be a politician

Singapore's politicians are among the highest paid in the world. The president draws a high annual pay (also known as the Privy Purse) of more than S$4.2 million (US$3.3 million). Just as attractive is the prime minister's annual salary of just over S$3.4 million (US$2.7 million) while a cabinet minister gets a pay of S$1.5 million (US$1.2 million) a year. Comparatively the President of the United States pulls in only US$400,000 annually.

The government believes that high salaries are necessary to attract the best talents and to prevent corruption. And because political leaders are expected to perform like CEOs, they should be paid like corporate honchos. The salaries of Singapore's ministers are determined by benchmarking to those of top earners in six professions.

were from Iraq, Marshall was educated in Britain, became a prisoner of war when the Japanese invaded Singapore, and later established himself as Singapore's best criminal defence attorney. He was elected as Singapore's first chief minister in 1955 but, with the rise of Lee Kuan Yew and the pap, soon found himself cast in the role of dissenter. In 1969, Lee and his government banned all trials by jury, putting a severe dent in Marshall's high-profile career. Marshall was among the very few in Singapore to openly oppose caning as a punishment for minor criminal offences. The year before his death he branded Lee a fascist.

Most Singaporeans live in public housing

Such a view in Singapore today is perhaps that of the minority. Full employment, bureaucratic efficiency, social stability and a continued high standard of living have pleased most residents, who are free to vote out the ruling party under Singapore's parliamentary system. The ruling party has promised to open the political process to the people and, by making Singapore a more cultured society, stem the brain drain of some of its most highly educated citizens to the West. How Singapore will shape itself to meet raised expectations in the 21st century remains an open question, one that may take the rise of another Stamford Raffles or Lee Kuan Yew to answer.

Historical landmarks

14th century Singapura (Sanskrit for 'Lion City') is named by Sang Nila Utama, a Sumatran prince.

15th century Singapore is made part of the Malay kingdom of Malacca.

1819 Sir Stamford Raffles makes Singapore a British trading post.

1824 Singapore is purchased by the British East India Company. It forms part of the Straits Settlements together with Malacca and Penang.

1867 The Straits Settlements become a British Crown Colony.

1869 Suez Canal opens and Singapore becomes an important stop along the main shipping route for rubber.

1942–5 Singapore is occupied by the Japanese army.

1946 The British make Singapore a Crown Colony.

1955 David Marshall heads the first elected government.

1959 Singapore achieves self-government; Lee Kuan Yew and the People's Action Party (PAP) control the new parliament.

1963 Singapore joins the Federation of Malaysia.

1965 Singapore separates from Malaysia and becomes an independent state. Lee Kuan Yew heads the new Republic of Singapore.

1990 Goh Chok Tong takes over from Lee Kuan Yew.

1998 The economy is affected by the Asian financial crisis, but recovers a year later.

2004 Lee Hsien Loong takes over as prime minister..

2005 The green light is given to legalise casino gambling. SR Nathan returns for his second term as president.

2006 The PAP wins 82 of 84 seats in the general elections.

2010 Singapore's first integrated resorts, Resorts World Sentosa and Marina Bay Sands, open. Singapore hosts the first Youth Olympic Games.

2011 In the general elections, ruling party PAP faces its worst results since independence in 1965, winning 60.1 percent of votes. S.R. Nathan steps down as president and Tony Tan is elected.

2012 The sprawling Gardens by the Bay are unveiled.

2015 Singapore to host the 28th Southeast Asian Games and the 8th ASEAN Para Games.

WHERE TO GO

Singapore can take days to explore. In addition to excellent eating and shopping, there are plenty of attractions well worth taking in. The leading sights are grouped here by district, with most located near the heart of the city and the Singapore River, which flows through it. Many of the older neighbourhoods and attractions have been modernised, but there are still some areas that have escaped renewal and offer a window on old Singapore.

SINGAPORE RIVER

A good place to begin exploration is the **Singapore River**. This was where Sir Thomas Stamford Raffles, Singapore's founder, and early traders and immigrants first landed. The mangrove swamps, sultans' palaces and floating skulls deposited by pirates are long gone, as are the junks and coolies. The river, now cleaned up, is lined by conservation shophouses painted in colourful hues and surrounded by colonial architectural gems.

North Bank

Raffles' Landing Site on the north bank of the river is where Sir Stamford Raffles first landed in 1819. The spot is marked by a white marble statue cast in 1972 from a bronze one that is a stone's throw away in front of the Victoria Theatre. Flanking the white statue is the **Asian Civilisations Museum ❶** (1 Empress Place; tel: 6332 7798; www.acm.org.sg; daily 10am–7pm, Fri until 9pm). Built as government offices in 1865, the stately neoclassical building now showcases an excellent collection of artefacts documenting the civilisations of East,

The supertrees found in the Gardens by the Bay

Singapore River runs past the Central Business District

Southeast, South and West Asia. You can easily spend a few hours viewing the well-curated displays here. Take a break from sightseeing and have a drink or bite at Empress Place, located at the river-facing side of the building.

Next to the museum is another ensemble of magnificent colonial architecture. The **Victoria Theatre** (9 Empress Place; tel: 6338 8283) and **Concert Hall** (11 Empress Place; tel: 6338 4401, closed for renovation until October 2014) were Singapore's old Town Hall and Queen Victoria Memorial Hall. The original bronze statue of Sir Stamford Raffles, which dates back to 1887, stands in front of the two buildings. Just behind is **The Arts House** (1 Old Parliament Lane; tel: 6332 6900; www.theartshouse.com.sg; Mon–Fri 10am–8pm, Sat 11am–8pm), built in 1827 as Singapore's courthouse and serving as the Parliament House from 1965 to 1999. It now has a 200-seat chamber staging arts performances, a visual arts gallery and an art-house cinema.

South Bank

From Empress Place Waterfront extends **Cavenagh Bridge**, built of iron rails from Scotland in 1869 to connect the financial and administrative districts that Raffles had envisioned. This pedestrian bridge leads to the skyscrapers of **Raffles Place**, the heart of Avi, which dictate the most propitious locations of the city's Western-style high-rises.

Next to Raffles Place is the lavish **Fullerton Hotel ❷** (1 Fullerton Square; tel: 6733 8388; www.fullertonhotel.com), built as the General Post Office in 1928. The hotel, with grand columns outside and a contemporary interior, stands on the site of Fort Fullerton, which guarded the entrance to Singapore from 1829 to 1873. The hotel's Post Bar is a firm favourite with workers from the CBD area.

Marina Bay

An underpass below the Fullerton emerges at **One Fullerton**, a waterfront dining and nightlife hub. At the north end of One Fullerton is the **Merlion Park**, which contains the Merlion statue – the city's iconic mascot with the head of a lion and the body of a fish. This 8m (26ft) -high sculpture was commissioned in 1972 by the Singapore Tourism Board as a welcome figure to visitors. It is de rigueur to come here to photograph the Merlion against the gleaming city skyline. At the other end of One Fullerton are several architecturally unique structures including Customs House, home to several trendy restaurants and bars; The Fullerton Pavilion, a floating dome structure housing the

River sculpture

A handful of public sculptures dot the Singapore River area. Of note are Fernando Botero's *Bird* and Salvador Dali's *Homage to Newton* outside and at the foyer of uob Plaza respectively. There are also bronze sculptures depicting life along the river in the early days.

famous Catalunya Spanish restaurant; and The Fullerton Bay Hotel, a sophisticated hotel with beautiful views of the bay.

Across the water is **Esplanade – Theatres on the Bay ❸** (1 Esplanade Drive; tel: 6828 8377; www.esplanade.com), the epicentre of Singapore's arts scene. Its unique architecture, resembling the husk of the thorny durian fruit Singaporeans love to eat, has been much debated. Inside are a 1,600-seat concert hall and a 2,000-seat theatre – both with exceptional acoustics. Local and international artists and groups perform year round.

You can take a **bumboat** or river taxi (tel: 6336 6119/111; www.rivercruise.com.sg; daily 9.15am–10.30pm) from any of the jetties near Raffles' Landing Site, Merlion Park, Boat Quay, Esplanade and Clarke Quay for a narrated tour. A bumboat ride offers an excellent view of the city skyline as the boat chugs into **Marina Bay ❹**, an inner harbour created by massive land reclamation projects that include Collyer Quay to the south, and the area to the north where the Esplanade and **Suntec City** stand.

One of the many 'engineering wonders' in this area is the 200m (656ft) **Sands Sky Park**, a unique structure designed by architect Moshe Safdie, which crowns the three Marina Bay Sands hotel towers. Perched on top of these towers are a sweeping 1.2-hectare (3 acre) tropical park with landscaped

Bay buzz

The reclaimed Marina Bay area bordering the waterfront is an exciting area. Located here are the Marina Bay Financial Centre, an extension of the CBD, and the lush Gardens by the Bay. Anchoring this area is the massive S$5 billion integrated resort, Marina Bay Sands (www.marinabay sands.com). This mega leisure, entertainment and hospitality complex features a casino, luxury hotel, convention facilities, theatres, and restaurants helmed by celebrity chefs.

gardens, an observation deck and an infinity pool with amazing views. It's not just about entertainment here – the integrated resort also boasts an **Art Science Museum** ❺ (tel: 6688 8826; daily 10am–10pm). The enormous lotus-shaped building houses galleries exhibiting art, science, media, technology, design and architecture. Another engineering masterpiece is the world's first double-helix curved bridge, which allows pedestrians to walk from Marina Bay Sands to the other side of the waterfront where luxury hotels are located. To the west of the East Coast Parkway lies **Gardens by the Bay** ❻ (18 Marina Gardens Drive; tel: 6420 6848; www.gardensbythebay.com.sg; outdoor gardens: daily 5am–2am, conservatories and OCBC Skyway: 9am–9pm; outdoor gardens free). The 101-hectare park, built on reclaimed land, features two energy-efficient conservatories: the Flower Dome and the Cloud Forest. The former's controlled environment replicates the cool-dry climate of Mediterranean regions, while the latter boasts the world's tallest indoor waterfall. There are also more than a dozen towering 'Supertrees' that offer shade in the day and glittering light displays at night. The OCBC Skyway that connects two of the Supertrees offers impressive views.

Along this waterfront is another of Singapore's top attractions, the **Singapore Flyer** ❼ (tel: 6333 3311; www.

The Singapore Flyer

singaporeflyer.com; daily 8.30am–10.30pm). At 165m (541ft), it is the world's second highest observation wheel, after one in Las Vegas. The ride, taking 30 minutes, affords stunning views of the city. At the foot of the wheel is a 1960s-themed food street, set up to lure local diners and tourists. Within walking distance is a large area where the Singapore Formula 1 night race takes place annually in September. Nearby, too, is Suntec City, a business, convention and shopping complex known for its colossal **Fountain of Wealth**.

Boat Quay and upriver

Raffles originally ordered the creation of five embankments along the Singapore River by reclamation. Collyer Quay and Raffles Quay were built south of the river's mouth; Boat Quay, Clarke Quay and Robertson Quay lined the river inland through the heart of the city.

Boat Quay is a great dining and drinking venue

Boat Quay ❽ runs on the southwest side of the river between the Cavenagh Bridge and Elgin Bridge. Completed in 1929 to connect the Chinese and Indian communities, it was a landfill project that handled most of Singapore's trade. The river's commercial traffic is now gone, but Boat Quay is enjoying a second lease of life with restaurants and drinking holes in its conservation shophouses, popular with tourists and executives from the nearby Raffles Place.

Upriver from Boat Quay, on the north bank, is **Clarke Quay ❾**, the site of scores of 19th-century godowns built by colonialists and Chinese merchants. Several of the latter became millionaires through their trading businesses at Clarke Quay. The old godowns have been converted into trendy restaurants and pubs.

Most tourists don't venture as far as **Robertson Quay**, a little further upriver, but it is a pleasant shoreline walk from Clarke and Boat quays. This former warehouse area is the largest of the three quays and is frequented by expats and residents who live nearby. The **Singapore Tyler Print Institute** (41 Robertson Quay; tel: 6336 3663; www.stpi.com.sg; Tue–Sat 10am–6pm; free) houses a fine collection of printed works, a printmaking workshop and a paper mill. In the vicinity are good restaurants, bars and cafés, the **Singapore Repertory Theatre** (20 Merbau Road; tel: 6733 8166; www.srt.com.sg).

CIVIC DISTRICT

For decades, visitors to downtown Singapore have referred to the area north of the lower Singapore River as the Colonial District, and for good reason. This is where many of the colonial-era buildings and museums stand. Raffles had assigned the north side of the river for the British from the beginning, ordering the building of offices, banks, hotels, churches and clubs there. He even built his house on the top of Fort Canning Hill. The leading colonial architects of the time were George

Coleman, who consulted with Raffles on many designs, and John Bidwell, who brought neo-Renaissance plans to the Raffles Hotel, the Goodwood Park Hotel, the Victoria Theatre and many other buildings. Fortunately, many of these buildings in what has been renamed the **Civic District**, roughly the area between the Dhoby Ghaut and City Hall MRT stations, have been preserved.

City Hall

Rising above the City Hall MRT Station and accessed via North Bridge Road in an expanse of greenery is **St Andrew's Cathedral** ❿ (tel: 6337 6104; www.livingstreams.org.sg;

Preservation and destruction

When Singapore achieved independence in 1965, the economy was in a shambles. Like every developing nation, Singapore put modernisation and economic progress on the front burner; anything that stood in the way, from historic neighbourhoods to colonial architecture, was simply razed. By the 1970s, Singapore was on its way to achieving spectacular prosperity, but it had obliterated much of its past and visitors complained that it lacked character and colour.

By the 1980s, Singapore began to heed its critics. Historic temples, office buildings, Peranakan mansions, shophouses and godowns were frequently spared demolition and restored with grace instead.

By the late 1980s, the government focused on four areas for conservation (Boat Quay, Little India, Kampong Glam and Chinatown). More areas have been added since. For some, these efforts at preservation have come too late; others felt the preservation schemes have too often been directed by commercial, rather than aesthetic, considerations. Have Singapore's conservation measures transformed the city into a Disneyesque museum, or have they rescued outstanding architectural treasures from neglect? You decide.

Mon–Sat 9am–5pm). A gazetted monument, the church owes its smooth white surface to the unique plaster that was used by Indian convict labourers. Called Madras *chunam*, it was made of egg white, eggshell, lime, sugar, coconut husk and water, and it gave the building a polished finish. This is the second place of worship on the premises. The original, which

St Andrew's Cathedral

was designed in Palladian style by Coleman, was twice struck by lightning and demolished in 1852. The present cathedral, in the style of an early Gothic abbey and designed by Ronald MacPherson, was consecrated in 1862. The gleaming white exterior contrasts with the dark pews inside, with sunlight filtering through the stained-glass windows in the morning.

If you exit the church premises onto St Andrew's Road and cross Colemen Street, you will come face to face with the **City Hall** (3 St Andrew's Road), built in ornate neoclassical style in 1929. This was where the Japanese surrendered to the British in 1945 and where Lee Kuan Yew declared Singapore's independence from British rule in 1959. Its grand staircase, with a backdrop of large Greek columns, is a favourite photography spot for wedding couples.

The **old Supreme Court**, built in 1939, stands next to the City Hall. It is one of Singapore's last classical edifices with Corinthian columns. It occupies the site of Hotel de L'Europe, once the city's most elegant place to stay, according to Rudyard Kipling and other travellers. The court has now moved into the shiny glass-and-steel **new Supreme Court** building (1 Supreme Court Lane) behind. There is an observation deck on the 8th floor and a gallery on level one that traces Singapore's legal history (tel: 6226 0644; both daily 8.30am–6pm; free). The City Hall and the old Supreme Court will be converted into a national art gallery by 2015 .

Across the street from these government buildings is a large field known as the **Padang** (Malay for 'field'), where Raffles planted the British flag and ordered the ground cleared. It has long been the site of cricket matches for the members-only **Singapore Cricket Club**, founded in 1852. The club building stands on one side of the Padang, where the Japanese military rounded up the entire European population of Singapore for interrogation in 1942.

Armenian Street

The **Armenian Church** ⑪ (60 Hill Street; tel: 6334 0141; http://armeniansinasia.org; daily 9am–6pm) stands at the head of Coleman Street. Built in 1835, the church is Singapore's oldest; it is also George Coleman's masterwork. Constructed using Indian convict labour, it served refugees fleeing the war between Russia and Turkey. The churchyard contains the graves of a few of Singapore's most famous Armenian residents: the Sarkies brothers, who built Raffles Hotel, and Agnes Joachim, who discovered the orchid that would be named as Singapore's national flower, the Vanda Miss Joaquim. Round the corner from the Armenian Church, at 39 Armenian Street, is the **Peranakan Museum** ⑫ (tel: 6332 7591; www.peranakanmuseum.org.sg; daily 10am–7pm, Fri until 9pm). The Peranakans (or Straits Chinese) have a hybrid culture that evolved through intermarriage between Chinese men and Malay women in the early days.

Also along this quiet stretch is **The Substation** (45 Armenian Street; tel: 6337 7535; www.substation.org), a centre for artistic experimentation and cutting-edge work, converted from a disused power station. It has a tiny theatre and an equally small gallery that connects to a charming garden overhung with trees. Located in the garden is **Timbre Music Bistro** (tel: 6338 8030; daily 6pm–late), an atmospheric nook where Singapore bands and musicians take to the stage nightly.

Fort Canning Park

Forming the western boundary of the Civic District is **Fort Canning Park** , which can be accessed via Canning Rise that adjoins Armenian Street, up a flight of stairs next to mica Building on Hill Street.

The hill, once the site of royal palaces built by Malay sultans, was known as Forbidden Hill (Bukit Larangan), for commoners were not allowed there. The ghosts of the sultans were believed to haunt the hill, the curse not broken until British resident William Farquhar cleared the summit and erected a cannon there for defence in the early 19th century. Raffles

Fort Canning Hill

built a bungalow on the hill in 1822, occupying it for almost a year. Until the British surrendered to the Japanese in World War II, the hill was a military command post.

Today Fort Canning Park has a well-marked trail that makes for a pleasant walk. Begin at the whitewashed Fort Canning Centre (currently undergoing renovation), a former army barracks. The oasis of green out front is a venue for arts and music events, such as the annual *Ballet Under The Stars* by the Singapore Dance Theatre, usually held in July. Hotel Fort Canning, to the west, is housed in a beautiful heritage military building constructed in 1926. Other attractions within the park include the **asean Sculpture Garden**, the original **fort gate** and a replica of the 19-hectare (47-acre) **spice garden** that Raffles established in 1822 as the 'experimental and botanical garden' of colonial Singapore. There are free guided walks on Saturday afternoons (4pm–5.30pm; tel: 6636 2393).

The main attraction is the **Battle Box** (51 Canning Rise; tel: 6333 0510; www.nparks.gov.sg), although this is currently closed for maintenance until further notice. This bomb-proof bunker with 22 rooms and corridors 9m (30ft) underground was where British Lt-General Percival decided to surrender to the Japanese (15 February 1942).

National Museum

National Museum
The **National Museum** (tel: 6332 5642; www.national museum.sg; daily 10am–6pm (History Gallery), 10am–8pm (Living Galleries)), at 93 Stamford Road, is housed in one of Singapore's most impressive colonial edifices. A modern glass-and-steel wing features a striking giant glass

Inside the Battle Box

rotunda on which images depicting Singapore's history are projected at night. The museum has also reinvented itself as a hip space to learn about history with its interactive displays and narratives. Look out for the Singapore History Gallery with 11 national treasures, from the Singapore Stone, a rock with inscriptions dating back to the 10th century, to 14th-century Majapahit gold ornaments from Fort Canning Hill. The museum also has an interesting line-up of performing and visual arts programmes.

Singapore Art Museum

Along Bras Basah Road is the **Singapore Art Museum** ⑮ (tel: 6332 3222; www.singaporeartmuseum.sg; Mon–Sun 10am–7pm, Fri 10am–9pm; free Fri 6–9pm). The colonial structure, dating from the early 1800s, formerly housed St Joseph's Institution, a school set up by Catholic missionaries. The museum's permanent collection is an excellent sampling of works by Southeast Asia's leading artists. It ranks among

Singapore Art Museum

the finest contemporary art museums in the region (past exhibitions have included works from New York's Guggenheim Museum). Even if not for the artworks, the museum is worth visiting just to see the splendidly restored chapel and the school hall, now called the glass hall. The latter features a colourful glass sculpture by American artist Dale Chihuly.

Chijmes

CHIJMES (30 Victoria Street; tel: 6337 7810; www.chij mes.com.sg) – pronounced 'chimes'– is a complex of build- ings within a walled enclosure, formerly the Catholic girls' school Convent of the Holy Infant Jesus, located at the corner of Victoria Street and North Bridge Road. These buildings, which may well be the most beautiful Christian architectural legacy in Singapore, have been painstakingly restored to their original glory. The chapel, dating from 1903, is the most mag- nificent. Designed by Father Charles Benedict Nain, a French priest, it is medieval in design and ornamentation. It is now used as a concert hall and a wedding venue.

The 'Gate of Hope' entrance along Bras Basah Road was once where the destitute and desperate left newborn babies in hope that the convent would adopt them. Today merrymak- ers – and not the impoverished – enter the convent gates as CHIJMES is now home to restaurants and bars, as well as a handful of boutiques and handicraft shops.

Opposite CHIJMES across Victoria Street is the oldest Roman Catholic church in Singapore, the **Cathedral of the**

Good Shepherd ('A' Queen Street; tel: 6337 2036; closed for restoration until 2016), built in 1846 in Renaissance style with six porticoed entrances and a high wooden ceiling.

The Raffles

Located diagonally across CHIJIMES is the **Raffles Hotel**  (1 Beach Road; tel: 6337 1886; www.raffles.com), perhaps the most famous hotel in Asia. It began as a small hotel in 1887 founded by the Armenian Sarkies brothers. The writer Joseph Conrad was among the first to check in, followed in 1889 by Rudyard Kipling, who praised the food but not the accommodation. The Sarkies then went on an upgrading rampage, adding the Tiffin Room, Palm Court and the Billiard Room by 1902.

Monarchs, celebrities and famous writers, including Charlie Chaplin, Somerset Maugham and John Lennon, have stayed at the Raffles. But by the 1990s the hotel was suffering from

The elegant Raffles Hotel

Doorman at Raffles Hotel

neglect and decay, leading the government to declare it a national monument and provide for a massive facelift. The restoration involved years of tracking down original plans and finding skilled craftsmen to repair and recreate the original fittings.

Nearly everyone who comes to Singapore visits the Raffles. Its **Bar & Billiard Room** is probably the most romantic spot for a drink, and the courtyard is good for open-air dining. And while the **Long Bar** may be nothing like the atmospheric original (despite ceiling fans and peanut shells on the floor), it is still a good place to knock back a Singapore Sling, the famous gin-based cocktail that was first concocted here in the early 1900s.

Exit the Raffles Hotel onto Seah Street to a quirky find. At No. 26 is the **Mint Museum of Toys** (tel: 6339 0660; www.emint.com; daily 9.30am–6.30pm), with a nostalgic collection of rare toys from all over the world spanning over 100 years.

CHINATOWN

Sir Thomas Stamford Raffles drew the outlines of Singapore's Chinatown in 1822, just after the first boatloads of immigrants from southern China landed at the mouth of the river. The Chinese found hard-labour jobs along the river; their fresh water source was a well on Spring Street, and gangs, triads and opium dens became a way of life. **Chinatown ⓱** then, as now, occupied a large area immediately southwest of the Singapore

River. The Hokkien traders settled along today's Telok Ayer and Amoy streets, the Teochew fishermen congregated near Boat Quay, and the Cantonese merchants built shophouses along Pagoda and Temple streets.

North Bridge Road and Eu Tong Sen Street are the main thoroughfares through the heart of Chinatown, lined by shopping arcades like the **People's Park Complex** (1 Park Road), which has fashion stores and old-style fabric tenants, and the **Yue Hwa Emporium** (70 Eu Tong Sen Street; tel: 6538 4222; www.yuehwa.com.sg; Sun–Fri 11am–9pm, Sat 11am–10pm) with all things Chinese, from silk to souvenirs. The latter occupies the building of the former Great Southern Hotel, once considered the grand old lady of Chinatown. Diagonally across Yue Hwa is **Chinatown Point** (www.chinatownpoint.com.sg), towering above the Chinatown MRT Station. There are many mid-priced food and fashion outlets as well as a few travel agencies. .

Chinatown

Chinatown Heritage Centre

Begin your exploration in Pagoda Street, where the **Chinatown Heritage Centre** ⑱ (No. 48; tel: 6221 9556; www.singaporechinatown.com.sg; daily 9am–8pm) is located in a conservation shophouse. It showcases the area's cultural heritage and includes a re-creation of the cramped living conditions of early residents.

Pagoda Street joins **South Bridge Road**, the traditional area for Cantonese merchants specialising in herbal medicines and gold jewellery. Flanking this road are several sights of interest to the visitor, including two sights that are not at all Chinese. The **Jamae Mosque** (218 South Bridge Road; tel: 6221 4165 daily 9.30am–6pm) has distinctive pagoda-like minarets rarely seen in mosque architecture. Its unique design was perhaps a gesture of deference to the predominantly Chinese neighbourhood. The mosque was constructed in 1826 by Muslim Chulia immigrants who came from South India's Coromandel Coast.

Adjacent to the mosque is **Sri Mariamman Temple** ⑲ (244 South Bridge Road; tel: 6223 4064; daily 9am–5pm, Wed 9.45am–5pm, Sun 9am–1.30pm). Dedicated to goddess Mariamman, who is known for curing serious illnesses, this is Singapore's most important and oldest Hindu temple, dating from 1827. Its *gopuram* tower is decorated with figures of

Love Potions

Aphrodisiacs are something of a Singapore obsession. **Eu Yan Sang Medical Hall** (269 South Bridge Road, opposite the Sri Mariamman Temple; tel: 6223 6333; www.euyansang.com.sg; Mon–Sat 8.30am–7pm) offers a selection of the best in Chinese love potions, from deer penis wine to seahorse tonic. Likewise, any other pharmacy in Chinatown worth its ginseng will stock a fertile line of sexual herbs, tonics and antlers to lift a flagging libido. Along **Arab Street**, Malay medicinal houses favour onions for prolonging sexual stamina. Indian pharmacists, relying on the Tantric traditions and the Kama Sutra, will boil asparagus and treacle in milk and ghee, spiced with liquorice. You'll find a storehouse of the ingredients used in Indian aphrodisiacs at the **Mustafa Centre** on Syed Alwi Road in Little India.

Display at the Chinatown Heritage Centre

Hindu gods. The interior is noted for its ceiling paintings and the temple is the site for the Thimithi ceremony (October/November) during which devotees walk on burning coals.

Chinatown streets

The best time to visit Chinatown is January/February when its streets are adorned with lights and bright-red decorations to usher in the Chinese New Year and when crowds throng its bazaar for New Year goodies. The **Chinatown Night Market** (daily 10am–10pm) has about 200 stalls lining Pagoda, Trengganu and Sago streets. A stroll down **Temple Street** takes one past Chinese souvenir shops (with lacquerware, silks, Tiger Balm ointments) to **Trengganu Street**, now an out-door street vendors' mall but previously an opera street with theatre stages and brothels.

Trengganu Street cuts through **Smith Street**, where you will find the fully pedestrianised **Chinatown Food Street**

Trengganu Street in Chinatown

(daily 11am–11pm). Post renovation, the stretch is now equipped with a massive glass shelter and fans to keep the area cool and comfortable for diners. There are six shophouse restaurants as well as 24 hawker stalls selling a huge range of local fare like Hokkien noodles, *char kway teow* (fried rice noodles), oyster omelette and barbecued chicken wings.

Trengganu Street ends at **Sago Street**, another colourful shopping area with Chinese medical halls, rattan weavers and pastry shops. Between Sago Street and Sago Lane is the **Buddha Tooth Relic Temple and Museum** (tel: 6220 0220; www.btrts.org.sg; daily 7am–7pm). Inspired by the Tang dynasty, this modern temple houses religious artworks and Buddhist texts. The temple's centrepiece is one dogged by much controversy – a sacred tooth belonging to the Buddha. Only taken out for viewing on Vesak Day and Chinese New Year, the tooth's authenticity has been questioned by several Buddhist scholars.

Tanjong Pagar District

From Sago Lane, turn right and walk to the corner of Tanjong Pagar and Neil roads, where the stately **Jinriksha Station** stands. Rickshaw coolies once parked their two-wheeled vehicles here. The station, built in 1903 in the classical style, is crowned by a dome. Jinrikshas were the main means of transport in Singapore in the early 1900s before they were replaced by three-wheeled trishaws in the 1940s. The rickshaw coolies lived around the station, renting beds in tiny cubicles in Chinatown.

Tanjong Pagar started out as a Malay fishing village. In the 1830s, the land around it was turned into a nutmeg plantation. The area became a thriving commercial hub, but by the 1960s, the neighbourhood had fallen into disrepair and would have met the wrecker's ball if it hadn't been for the government's conservation drive. It soon became an archetype for how the remainder of historic Singapore would be restored. Today the **Tanjong Pagar Conservation District** has over 190 meticulously restored shophouses, in pastel hues with wooden window shutters and high-beamed ceilings, along Neil Road, Murray Terrace, Craig Road and Duxton Hill Road. Offices, restaurants and pubs now call these shophouses home.

Further down along Neil Road past Kreta Ayer Road is the once notorious **Keong Saik Road**, a red-light district that has now been gentrified. Many of the area's splendid shophouses in the Chinese Baroque architectural style have been restored and converted into boutique hotels such as **Hotel 1929** (No. 50; tel: 6347 1929; www.hotel 1929.com), which is largely responsible for making this

Snack time

A must-try in Chinatown is *bak kwa*, a delicious sweet barbecued meat. Just follow your nose to one of the many shops selling this addictive snack. The most popular are Lim Chee Guan at 203 New Bridge Road and Bee Cheng Hiang at 69 Pagoda Street.

strip hip. Trendy bars and restaurants now share space with brothels and scruffy coffeeshops.

Singapore City Gallery

Opposite the Jinriksha Station across Maxwell Road is a local favourite, **Maxwell Food Centre**, one of Singapore's oldest hawker centres. Snaking queues are a regular sight at lunchtime.

Beside the food centre across Kadayanallur Street is the ura Centre with the **Singapore City Gallery** (45 Maxwell Road; tel: 6321 8321; www.ura.gov.sg/gallery; Mon–Sat 9am–5pm), whose key attraction is a massive model of the city. Spread over two storeys are exhibits, interactive displays and touch-screen terminals as well as audio-visual programmes about this efficient city.

Kadayanallur Street leads uphill to **Ann Siang Road** but not before passing **The Scarlet**, a swanky boutique hotel with

Streetside calligrapher in Chinatown

dramatic interiors (33 Erskine Road; tel: 6511 3333; www.
thescarlethotel.com). Further up is another luxury boutique
hotel, **The Club Hotel** (28 Ann Siang Road; tel: 6808 2188;
http://theclub.com.sg), housed in a 1900 heritage building.

Club Street

Ann Siang Road adjoins **Club Street**, once home to trade
associations and the haunt of letter-writers for hire. The area
is filled with finely restored shophouses (as well as a few colourful unrestored specimens). Their architectural style is not
entirely Chinese. The carved decorations and swinging *pintu
pagar* doors are Malay in origin, the Georgian windows and
Art Deco touches are European, and the tiled roofs are strictly
in the Chinese style. This area is today lined with fashionable
bars and bistros as well as two established Italian restaurants:
Senso Ristorante and Bar (21 Club Street; tel: 6224 3534;
www.senso.sg) and **Da Paolo** (80 Club Street; tel: 6224 7081;
www.dapaolo.com.sg).

Telok Ayer Street

Club Street rises and dips into Upper Cross Street, the location of **Far East Square** and **China Square Central**, whose
eateries and cafés are often filled with office workers during
lunch time. Far East Square is worth a stroll for its interesting
shophouses and entrance gates that represent the five elements
that make up the Chinese universe.

On the east side of Far East Square is **Telok Ayer Street**,
which has a cluster of national monuments, beginning with
the **Fuk Tak Chi Museum** (No. 76; tel: 6532 7868; www.
fareastsquare.com.sg; daily 10am–10pm; free). Formerly the
Fuk Tak Chi Temple, built by Hakka and Cantonese immigrants in 1824 and dedicated to Tua Pek Kong, the Taoist God
of Prosperity, the museum has a collection of 200 artefacts,
including a Chinese gold belt, abacus board and even a rental

Far East Square's 'Fire' gate

expiry notice, from early Chinatown residents. A little down the street is **Ying Fo Fui Kun** (No. 98; www.yingfofuikun.org.sg; Mon–Fri 9am–5pm, Sat 9am–noon; free), a Hakka clanhouse established in 1822, with traditional Chinese architectural elements such as carved beams and pillars. Further along are three places of worship. First up is the **Nagore Durgha Shrine** (No. 140; http://singaporenagoredargah.com), built between 1828 and 1830 by Muslims from southern India. Designated a national monument in 1974, but later closed due to concerns about its structure, the building finally reopened in 2011 as an Indian-Muslim heritage centre.

Thian Hock Keng Temple

Beside the shrine is **Telok Ayer Green**, a tiny park with life-sized bronze figures depicting scenes from the past. Steps away is the **Thian Hock Keng Temple** ⑳, the Temple of Heavenly Bliss (No. 158; tel: 6423 4616; www.thianhockkeng.com.sg; daily 7.30am–5.30pm), built between 1839 and 1842 by the first Chinese immigrants, who dedicated this elaborate shrine to their protector, Ma Chu Poh, Goddess of the Sea. It has granite pillars from China, blue tiles from Holland and cast-iron railings from Scotland. Although the main altar is Taoist, a rear chamber is dedicated to Guan Yin, the Buddhist Goddess of Mercy. The last temple on Telok Ayer Street is **Al-Abrar Mosque** (No. 192; daily 11.30am–9pm), known as the Indian (or Chulia) Mosque.

Art and design

Follow the road past the **Telok Ayer Chinese Methodist Church** on your left. Cut through Telok Ayer Park to the red dot Traffic building for a stopover at the **red dot design museum** (28 Maxwell Road; tel: 6327 8027; www.museum. red-dot.sg; Mon, Tue and Fri 11am–6pm, Sat–Sun until 8pm). Run by the German body that presents the prestigious red dot design award, the museum exhibits sleek products from around the world. The **MAAD (Market of Artists and Designers) flea market** (first Friday of the month, 5pm–midnight) here offers original works by young artists and designers.

LITTLE INDIA

Among the first Indian settlers were 120 assistants and soldiers who sailed to Singapore in 1819 with Raffles. They first congregated in Chulia Street, the original Indian quarter. But as cattle raising expanded along the Rochor River to the north, Indians settled in an area bisected by Serangoon Road, which is now known as **Little India** ㉑. Hindus are in the majority among Indians here and Tamil Muslims are well represented, but Chinese make up almost three quarters of Little India's population. This is perhaps Singapore's most colourful downtown neighbourhood with lively backstreets and a strong ethnic flavour.

Serangoon Road

For a walking tour of Little India, start at the **Little India Arcade** (48 Serangoon Road) between Campbell Lane and Hastings Road, opposite the fresh-produce market **Tekka**

Centre (665 Buffalo Road). The arcade has several shops selling saris and *cholis* (short-waisted blouses) as well as medicines, betel nuts, carvings, brassware and more. A branch of one of Singapore's most famous South Indian restaurants, the **Banana Leaf Apolo** (see page 109), is located here.

From Little India Arcade you can wander up Serangoon Road and explore its colourful side streets. Five-foot ways, which are covered corridors that front shophouses, run along **Campbell Lane**; shops here sell woodcarvings, furniture, musical instruments and flower garlands. **Dunlop Street** has backpacker inns as well as small grocery stores. A few blocks down at 41 Dunlop Street (near the Perak Street junction) is the **Abdul Gafoor Mosque** (tel: 6295 4209; daily 5am–9.30pm). Most Singaporean Indians are Hindu, but Muslim Indians congregate here every Friday. You can visit the mosque (except for the prayer hall) if you are dressed respectfully. The present brick structure,

Browsing in Little India

completed in 1907, features a blend of South Indian and Moorish architectural elements such as arches, onion-shaped domes and ornate ornamentation.

Day of rest

On Sundays, throngs of workers from the Indian subcontinent hang out in Little India on their rest day. Traffic can slow to a crawl, and the streets and shops are packed to the gills.

If you are feeling peckish, stop at the vegetarian restaurant **Komala Vilas** (see page 109) for a meal of *thosai* (rice-flour pancakes). Returning to Serangoon Road, take a brief detour down Cuff Road to **Ashaweni Mills** (No. 2 Cuff Road; tel: 6299 3726; Mon–Sat 8am–1pm and 2–5pm). It is one of the last remaining traditional spice grinders in Singapore, where the freshest mixes of spices, flours and betel nuts are custom ground.

Sri Veeramakaliamman Temple

A little further up Serangoon Road, next to Belilios Road, is the **Sri Veeramakaliamman Temple** (141 Serangoon Road; tel: 6295 4538; daily 8am–noon and 4–9pm), constructed by Bengalis in 1855. This is one of Singapore's finest Hindu shrines. Dedicated to Kali, the Hindu Goddess of Power, it is packed with devotees on the Hindu holy days of Tuesdays and Fridays. They often break a coconut before entering to denote the breaking of their ego. Cracked shells are tossed into the aluminium receptacles under the *gopuram* tower. The interior is interesting for several Hindu symbols it employs: fresh coconut and mango leaves above the entrance are for purity and welcome; the lotus represents human striving for spiritual perfection; the banana offerings indicate abundance.

Sri Srinivasa Perumal Temple

Near the Farrer Park MRT Station, at 397 Serangoon Road, is another national monument, the **Sri Srinivasa Perumal**

Sri Srinivasa Perumal Temple

Temple ㉒ (tel: 6298 5771; daily 6.30am–noon and 6–9pm). Dating from 1855, it has a vast prayer hall that honours Krishna (also known as Perumal), one of the incarnations of Vishnu, the supreme Hindu god. The temple is topped by a five-tier *gopuram* tower, donated by P. Govindasamy Pillai, an early Indian migrant made good.

Buddhist temples

On nearby Race Course Road, which runs parallel to the west of Serangoon Road, is the **Sakya Muni Buddha Gaya Temple ㉓** (No. 366; tel: 6294 0714; daily 8am–4.45pm), better known as the Temple of 1,000 Lights. This Buddhist shrine, maintained by Thai monks, is one of the most popular religious shrines in Singapore. Its centrepiece is the seated Buddha statue, 15m (49ft) tall and weighing 305kg (300 tons). It is surrounded by bulbs that light up every time a donation is made. Several Hindu statues and two bright yellow tigers are posted as guards outside.

The temple across the road, at 371 Race Course Road, is **Leong San Buddhist Temple** (Dragon Mountain Temple; tel: 6298 9371; daily 6am–5.30pm), a less fanciful place of worship that dates back to the late 1800s, dedicated to Guan Yin, the Goddess of Mercy. It also has an image of Confucius at its altar and is thAus popular with parents who bring their children to pray for success in examinations.

KAMPONG GLAM

Named after the *gelam* trees that once grew here, the **Kampong Glam** district (north of the Civic District and the Singapore River) was the historic seat of the Malay sultans. It was settled in the early days by Muslims from the Malay Peninsula and the Bugis from Indonesia. Even today this neighbourhood has maintained a Malay character.

Arab Street

Arab Street ㉔ is the traditional home of Singapore's textile dealers and there are still many small silk and batik stores as well as sarong shops and tailors here. Leather goods, caneware, fishing gear and shiny metalwork are also for sale in the shophouses and make for an interesting browse. Go early as most shops close after 5pm.

Sultan Mosque

Kampong Glam's leading attraction is the **Sultan Mosque** ㉕ (3 Muscat Road; tel: 6293 4405; www.sultanmosque.org. sg; Mon–Sun 9.30am–noon and 2–4pm, Fri 2.30–4pm), located between Arab Street and North Bridge Road at the end of Bussorah Street. It is an impressive structure, topped with a massive onion-shaped golden dome and corner minarets. A national monument that dates back to 1924, this is Singapore's largest mosque; visitors are welcome to view (but not enter) its grand prayer hall.

The grand Sultan Mosque

In a fashion and accessories store on Haji Lane

Malay Heritage Centre

The **Malay Heritage Centre** (85 Sultan Gate; tel: 6391 0450; www.malayheritage.org.sg; grounds: Tue–Sun 8am–8pm, Fri–Sat 8am–10pm, museum: Tue–Sun 10am–6pm) is housed in the large compound of **Istana Kampong Gelam**, the former residence of the son of the first sultan of Singapore, dating back to the 1840s.

To the left of the compound's main gate is the Yellow Mansion or **Gedung Kuning**, the former home of Tengku Mahmoud, grandson of Sultan Hussein. Malay entrepreneur and philanthropist Haji Yusoff bought Gedung Kuning in 1912 and his family owned the place until 1999 when the Singapore Government acquired it.

Kampong Glam Shopping

At 44 Kandahar Street is **Bumbu** (tel: 6392 8628; Tue–Sun 11am–3pm and 6–10pm), a Thai-Indonesian restaurant filled with an eclectic collection of rare antiques sourced from various Singaporean homes. Head back to **Bussorah Mall** for a spot of souvenir shopping. **Jamal Kazura Aromatics Store** (21 Bussorah Street; tel: 6293 3320; www.jamalkazura.com) has a fine display of decanters and alcohol-free perfumes for sale, and **Habib Leather & Crafts** (44 Bussorah Street; tel: 6291 3012) sells handicrafts and leather goods.

Continue down on **Haji Lane**, where the old mixes with the new and funky. This stretch is lined with independent boutiques such as **Salad** (No. 25/27; tel: 6299 5805) and **Dulcetfig** (No. 41; tel: 6396 5648), plus a cool **Tokyobike** bicycle shop (No.38; tel: 6299 5048) and a number of small cafés.

More historic mosques

Right at the corner of Jalan Sultan and Victoria Street is the **Malabar Jamaath Mosque** (471 Victoria Street; tel: 6294 3862; www.malabar.org.sg; daily 10am–noon and 2–4pm), famous for its blue tile work. Northeast of the Sultan Mosque, at 4001 Beach Road, is the **Hajjah Fatimah Mosque** (tel: 6297 2774; daily 10am–6pm), built in 1846 by the Malay wife of a Bugis merchant as a private residence. Its remarkable architecture mixes European and Chinese influences and it has a Malay-style minaret that resembles the spire of a cathedral. The minaret is off the plumb, leading some to dub it the 'leaning tower of Singapore'.

Bugis

Bugis Street, south of the Arab Street area, was Singapore's most notorious after-dark hangout

Drinking spots

Kampong Glam has several hip bars worth checking out. **Blu Jaz** (11 Bali Lane, tel: 6292 3800; www.blujaz. net) features evening jam sessions by local musicians. **Maison Ikkoku** (20 Kandahar Street; tel: 6294 0078; www.maison-ikkoku. net) is famous for its bespoke cocktails.

Bugis Street Market

until it was razed in 1985 to make way for the Bugis MRT station. Now, in place of a street internationally renowned for prostitution and drag queens, there is **Bugis Junction**, a shopping mall with a glassed-over air-conditioned shopping street and the adjoining hotel, InterContinental Singapore (80 Middle Road; tel: 6338 7600; www.ihg.com). Next to the hotel is the stark-white **National Library** (100 Victoria Street; tel: 6332 3255; www.nl.sg; daily 10am–9pm; free). It houses a reference library, restful outdoor gardens, a café, an art exhibition space and the Drama Centre performing arts theatre. Linking Bugis Junction via an overhead bridge is Bugis+, a mall targeted at the younger clientele.

Across Victoria Street is the lively **Bugis Street Market** ㉖ in the Bugis Village complex. Crammed with over 600 stalls, the market offers value finds such as look-alike Oakleys, cheap, fashionable streetwear and hawker food.

Waterloo Street

Follow Rochor Road by the side of the Bugis Village complex and turn into the pedestrianised section of **Waterloo Street** ㉗. On any given day, this area teems with people who come to pray at the Chinese **Kwan Im Thong Hood Cho**

Temple (No.178; tel: 6337 3965; daily 6am–6pm) and the Hindu **Sri Krishnan Temple** (No.152; tel: 6337 7957; daily 6am–2.30pm, 5.30–9pm).

The Buddhist Goddess of Mercy, Guan Yin, presides in the former. Built in 1895 and refurbished in 1982, the temple is a highlight not for its architecture but rather for the glimpses of colourful local life it offers. Pensive supplicants inside the temple kneel before the goddess in prayer. Some shake containers with numbered bamboo fortune sticks until one falls out, then consult with the fortune tellers who stake out stalls outside along with the traditional medicine and flower sellers. From lottery numbers to prospects for offspring, the goddess tries to unravel everything about the future.

Sculpture Square (tel: 6333 1055; www.sculpturesq.com.sg; gallery Mon–Fri 11am–7pm, closed on weekends, but subject to exhibition opening hours; free) is housed in a 19th-century church building at the corner of Waterloo Street and Middle Road. It presents interesting three-dimensional art exhibitions.

ORCHARD ROAD

The **Orchard Road** ㉘ area, roughly from the beginning of Plaza Singapura near the Dhoby Ghaut MRT Station all the way to the end of Tanglin Road near the Botanic Gardens, is Singapore's best known shopping and dining district, though it has some sights worth seeing too. The name of this glitzy road goes back to the 1840s when Captain William Scott established his nutmeg and pepper plantation on the slopes. Tigers roamed the hills along Orchard Road until 1846; fifty years later, the land was tamed and some of Singapore's richest families had built their estates and terrace homes here.

The most notable cluster of these historic residences is on **Emerald Hill** ㉙, the site of one of Singapore's first and most impressive preservation projects. A stroll up Emerald Hill

Road from Peranakan Place is a walk into Singapore's colonial past. The terrace houses were built between 1902 and 1930 on the site of a nutmeg farm using a plethora of Malay, Chinese and European styles. The original owners were wealthy Peranakan, a mixed race that evolved through intermarriage between immigrant Chinese men and local Malay women from the 17th to 19th centuries. Pastel hues, fancy plaster work, ornate grills, shuttered windows, bat-shaped openings, tiled overhangs and carved wood characterise many of these graceful exteriors. Among the houses are a few galleries, restaurants and pubs, which allow a glimpse of the colonial-period interiors, but most of the restored terrace houses and shophouses are private residences. The carved swing doors (*pintu pagar*) are designed for ventilation and privacy.

Orchard Road is also the address of the **Istana**, the Singapore president's official residence. In the late 1860s Indian convicts did the heavy work on this government estate, which is closed to visitors except on public holidays such as Chinese New Year's Day, Hari Raya Puasa, Labour Day, Deepavali and National Day (www.istana.gov.sg). If you are there on the first Sunday of the month, you can catch the changing of the guard at the gates at 6pm.

Orchard Road

Further away but more accessible is the **Goodwood Park Hotel** (22 Scotts Road; tel: 6737 7411; www.good woodparkhotel.com), a national landmark built in 1900 as the Teutonia Club for German colonialists. Resembling a Rhineland castle with an eight-sided Bavarian tower, it was occupied by the Japanese during the war and

Chinese Baroque houses on Emerald Hill

served as the War Crimes Court later. Celebrities who have spent the night here include Anna Pavlova and John Wayne.

GEYLANG SERAI AND KATONG

When the British transformed Singapore into a trading colony, many Malays took up residence in **Geylang Serai** ③, east of the city centre. The district still has a strong Malay character, complete with old bungalows, terrace houses and Peranakan shophouses, especially along Joo Chiat and Koon Seng roads near the Paya Lebar MRT Station. Singapore's largest red-light district and a cluster of 'love hotels' are located in the *lorong* (alleys) here. Here as well is the colourful **Geylang Serai Market**, located in a new double-storey building on Jalan Turi that was designed to simulate the rustic quality of the old Malay kampong houses. This market is at its busiest during the Ramadan month and just before Hari Raya Puasa.

Katong

North of Geylang Serai, further along Joo Chiat Road, is the **Katong** ③ suburb area. It is historically the heart of the Peranakan community and many of the shophouses here, combining Chinese, Peranakan and European architectural styles, have been conserved. Katong is also a foodie's haven, where you can find some of the best Peranakan restaurants in Singapore. The main spine to explore is East Coast Road. You can spend a day just sampling the many delicious offerings, from the famous spicy Katong *laksa* noodle dish (try one of the stalls at the corner of Ceylon and East Coast Road) to *kaya* (traditional coconut custard jam) toast at the nostalgic **Chin Mee Chin Confectionery** (204 East Coast Road; tel: 6345 0419; Tue–Sun 8.30am–4pm) and homemade rice dumplings at **Kim Choo Kueh Chang** (109 East Coast Road; tel: 6741 2125; www.kimchoo.com).

East Coast Seafood Centre

To see precious collections of Peranakan family heirlooms, intricately beaded slippers and jewellery, head to **Katong Antique House** (208 East Coast Road; tel: 6345 8544; Tue–Sun 11am–6.30pm, by appointment only) and **Rumah Bebe** (113 East Coast Road; tel: 6247 8781; www.rumah bebe.com; Tue–Sun 9.30am–6.30pm).

East Coast

Many people come to the East Coast for recreation (watersports, cycling, jogging and roller-blading) and dining. The **East Coast Seafood Centre**, housing restaurants such as **Red House** (see page 113), **Jumbo** (tel: 6442 3435; www. jumboseafood.com.sg) and **Long Beach** (tel: 6448 3636; www.longbeachseafood.com.sg), is incredibly popular, especially for chilli crab. Nearby is the **East Coast Lagoon Food Village** where hawker stalls roll out good, cheap local fare.

ZOOS, PARKS AND GARDENS

Some of Singapore's top attractions are found outside the urbanised centres and downtown Singapore. These include the island's world-renowned zoos, a park devoted to birds, and several nature reserves, which form a much appreciated counterweight to the city-state's urban landscape.

Singapore Botanic Gardens

The **Singapore Botanic Gardens** ㉜ (1 Cluny Road; tel: 6471 7138/6471 7361; www.sbg.org.sg; daily 5am–midnight; free), just west of Orchard Road, is the nearest major green preserve to the downtown district. The 67-hectare (166-acre) site of gardens and jungle forests was opened in 1859.

A path begins at Swan Lake, surrounded by palms and rubber trees, then leads past an 1860 bandstand and a topiary garden. The 1.5-hectare (3.7-acre) **Evolution Garden** traces life

Chinese Garden pavilions

on earth from 4,600 million years ago till the present day with live exhibits and plant replicas.

A must-visit is the **National Orchid Garden** (daily 8.30am–7pm), located within the Botanic Gardens, which claims to have the world's largest display of Singapore's signature blooms. It has over 1,000 spices and 2,000 hybrids of orchids, including Singapore's national flower, the purple Vanda Miss Joaquim, which was first discovered in 1893 by an Armenian immigrant, Agnes Joachim. There are also numerous 'vip' orchids, named after the many dignitaries who have visited Singapore. Located within this garden is the **Cool House**, which encloses a montane tropical forest.. Families can also visit the Jacob Ballas Children's Garden (Tue–Sun 8am–7pm), designed to help kids under 12 discover more about plants and nature through fun-filled play and exploration. Back at the **Visitor's Centre** (tel: 6471 7361), pick up a gift at the souvenir shop or have a bite at the alfresco café, Casa Verde (tel: 6467 7326).

Chinese and Japanese Gardens

Gardens of a different order are maintained at the **Chinese Garden** and **Japanese Garden** (1 Chinese Garden Road; tel: 6261 3632/1800-5687000; Chinese Garden daily 6am–11pm, Bonsai Garden 9am–5pm, Japanese Garden 6am–7pm; free). The Chinese Garden reflects several classical styles and has twin pagodas, arched bridges, an extensive *bonsai* display, elaborate rock works, a teahouse and even a marble boat like the one in Beijing's Summer Palace gardens. The garden is decorated with colourful lanterns in September/October for the annual Mid-Autumn Festival. From the Chinese Garden visitors can cross a bridge into the Japanese Garden with its carefully raked Zen rock gardens, stone lanterns, pavilions and pools.

Haw Par Villa

The most Chinese of Singapore's theme parks is **Haw Par Villa**, also known as Tiger Balm Gardens (262 Pasir Panjang Road; tel: 6872 2780; daily 9am–7pm; free). This park was opened in 1937 by local millionaire Aw Boon Haw, who built a mansion for his younger brother, Aw Boon Par, on the summit. The Aws made a vast fortune that was based, in large part, on sales of the famous Tiger Balm ointment. The Japanese destroyed the mansion during their occupation (1942–5) and it was never replaced, but the park itself was rebuilt.

Dragon slayer at Haw Par Villa

The amusement park lining the slopes below the villa is lined with garish and often grotesque statuary, telling stories from classical Chinese mythology, literature and folklore. The statues originally

See over 20 duck species at Jurong Bird Park

numbered over a thousand and there were scores of colourful and striking tableaux showing fantastic heroes and villains representing aspects of good and evil, engaged in the primal struggles of life and death.

Jurong Bird Park

The largest bird park in Southeast Asia, **Jurong Bird Park** ❸❸ (2 Jurong Hill; tel: 6265 0022; www.birdpark. com.sg; daily 8.30am–6pm) is located on 20 hectares (]50 acres) of parkland far west of downtown. More than 5,000 birds, representing 400 species, reside here. Its Southeast Asian hornbill collection is the largest in the world. Also the largest in the world is a 30m (98ft) -high artificial waterfall at the end of a walk-in aviary, where 1,500 birds fly freely.

It is best to arrive early before the heat gets too much. The park can be explored on foot, but there is a panorail (charge) that links the myriad displays. Among the more notable displays are the **Southeast Asian Birds Aviary**, where a tropical thunderstorm is simulated at noon, the **World of Darkness** nocturnal house, where snowy owls, night herons and kiwis can be observed in darkness, and the **Lory Loft**, another free flight aviary and the largest of its kind in the world. Built to simulate Australia's vast rural landscape, visitors can step onto the boardwalks and bridges suspended at a height of 12m (39ft) and watch the 1,000 free-flying Lory birds at treetop level.

Other attractions include the **Parrot Paradise** with the park's most colourful and friendly residents, **The Riverine**, offering a river's edge view of over 20 duck species fishing and nesting, and the **Pelican Cove**, where visitors can view underwater feeding of pelicans. There are also entertaining shows such as the High Flyers Show with cockatoos, pelicans and hornbills at the Pools Amphitheatre (daily 11am and 3pm), and the Kings of the Skies at the Hawk Walk (daily 10am and 4pm). Those who enjoy a good chat and Asian buffet meal can look out for Lunch with Parrots at the Songbird Terrace (noon–2pm).

Bukit Timah Nature Reserve

The **Bukit Timah Nature Reserve** ❸ (177 Hindhede Drive; tel: 1800 6468 5736; www.nparks.gov.sg; daily 6am–7pm; free), located in the northern part of the island, is easily reached by taking a taxi.

This spacious park, occupying 163 hectares (403 acres), harbours Singapore's largest surviving virgin lowland rainforest,

The feather in Singapore's cap

Although a concrete island of high-rises, Singapore has more than 350 species of birds to delight even the most casual bird-watcher. Early morning, around 7am, is prime spotting time. A good place to start a bird-watching expedition is at the Visitor Centre in the Bukit Timah Nature Reserve, where illustrated field guides are for sale. The Sungei Buloh Nature Park on the northwestern coast has observation blinds by mangroves where there's a breeding colony of herons in residence from August to March. Pulau Ubin, with its mangroves and rainforests, is home to parakeets, owls, kingfishers and hornbills. And from September to March, the white cattle egret takes its winter holiday in Singapore, arriving from as far north as Japan and as far west as France.

Bukit Timah Nature Reserve

native vegetation that once covered most of the island. Bukit Timah is a marvellous place to hike, with a series of well-marked trails winding through the hillsides. Bukit Timah is the name of the park's summit, the highest point in Singapore at a modest 164m (538ft).

Bukit Timah boasts more tree species than the whole of North America. The towering tropical trees provide a canopy for palms, rattans and over 80 species of fern. Flying lemurs, long-tailed macaques, pangolins (spiny anteaters), mouse deer, giant forest ants, banded woodpeckers and tit babblers are sometimes heard but not often seen.

The Visitor Centre (daily 8.30am–6pm) at the park entrance has hiking maps and an exhibition on the park's ecosystem. An uphill hike from the centre to the Summit Hut, with its picnic shelter and lookout on stilts, takes under 30 minutes. The four main walking trails (and side trails) lead to valleys and large quarries. There is also a 6km (4-mile) biking trail.

MacRitchie Reservoir Park

The **MacRitchie Reservoir Park** (tel: 1800 471 7300; www.nparks.gov.sg; daily 7am–7pm), located in the Central Catchment Nature Reserve along Lornie Road, is another scenic spot for nature lovers. Boardwalks and walking trails, ranging from 3 to 11km (2 to 7 miles), skirt the edge of the reservoir and head through the flourishing forest. The **TreeTop Walk** (tel: 1800 471 7300; www.nparks.gov.sg; Tue–Fri 9am–5pm, Sat–Sun 8.30am–5pm; free) offers good views of the forest canopy from dizzying heights of up to 25m (82ft). This 250m (820ft) -long suspension bridge connects the two highest points in the reservoir park. To get there, you must first hike through a 4.5km (3-mile) nature trail. The TreeTop Walk is especially popular at weekends, and with only 30 people allowed on the bridge at any one time, the wait to get on can be long. Go on a weekday to avoid the crowds.

Singapore Zoo

The **Singapore Zoo** ❸❺ on 80 Mandai Lake Road (tel: 6269 3411; www.zoo.com.sg; daily 8.30am–6pm), north of downtown, houses over 2,800 animals from 300 species (29 percent of which are threatened) on its 28 hectares (69 acres). Its 'open zoo' concept sets it apart from other zoos. Cleverly concealed features, including moats, cascading streams and vegetation, help serve as barriers, although a few glass-fronted enclosures are employed for species that can leap over walls. Some 'lucky' animals, including langurs, lemurs and tamarins, are allowed to roam freely around the zoo.

Not to be missed are the animal shows, staged six times daily in selected areas. Most are held in the Shaw Foundation Amphitheatre, where sea lions, reptiles and primates take their turns on stage. The elephant shows (daily 11.30am and 3.30pm) take place at the Elephants of Asia enclosure. An animal show specially designed to entertain children gets under way at the Rainforest Kidzworld Amphitheatre (daily 11am and 4pm). Note, too, that many animals, from lions and jaguars to monkeys and Komodo dragons, are fed on a regular schedule (times posted at the zoo entrance) and this can often lead to exciting impromptu shows. Even the tigers are likely to take a plunge in their pool when the feeding crew arrives.

The zoo also provides a splendid opportunity to have a meal in close proximity to the animals. If you fancy having a **Jungle Breakfast** (daily 9–10.30am) among orang-utans (the zoo's colony is the largest in the world) and other wildlife, book a place on the terrace at Ah Meng Restaurant in advance. Or get to feed some rare Hamadryas baboons when you hop on a buggy with a knowledgeable guide for the hour-long, personalised **Wild Discover Tour** (charge) into the heart of the forest.

To avoid the crowds, visit the zoo in the morning on a weekday. If you are combining a visit with the Night Safari next

Orangutan, pongo pygmaeus, Singapore Zoo

door, take your zoo tour in the afternoon, three to four hours before the 6pm closing time and then walk over to the Night Safari for dinner before the guided tram tours commence at 7.30pm. The zoo and the Night Safari are crowded all day every day, as these are two of Singapore's top attractions.

River Safari

Asia's first and only river-themed wildlife park, **River Safari** ㊱ (80 Mandai Lake Road; tel: 6269 3411; www.riversafari. com.sg; daily 9am–6pm) is home to over 6,000 aquatic and land animals, including 42 endangered species. The highlight is the Giant Panda Forest, which houses two giant pandas from China. Take a 'river adventure' down the Mississippi, Congo, Nile, Ganges, Murray, Mekong and Yangtze rivers, and visit the Squirrel Monkey Forest and Amazon Flooded Forest. This park also houses the world's largest freshwater aquarium.

Night Safari

The world's first night zoo, Singapore's **Night Safari** ㊲ (80 Mandai Lake Road; tel: 6269 3411; www.nightsafari.com.sg; daily 7.30pm–midnight) is the island nation's top attraction. Covering 40 hectares (99 acres), it is a completely different experience. Beginning at dusk (7.30pm), a series of trams with witty English-speaking narrators aboard, encircles the eight geographical zones on a paved road. Passengers can disembark to take a closer look at the animals in their open enclosures by following one of three walking trails (Fishing Cat, Leopard and Forest Giants).

Set in a dense tropical forest, the Night Safari is a subtly lit preserve inhabited by more than 2,500 animals from about 130 species found in Asia, Africa and South America. More than 90 percent of the animals in the wild are nocturnal, so this is a chance to see how the animals behave after the heat and sunlight have vanished.

Perhaps the most entertaining creatures are the fishing cats, which are slightly larger than domestic felines. These take the plunge to capture trout in a small stream just inches from the pedestrian bridge that passes through their wooded area. The focused, incandescent lighting used to illuminate the animals makes everything visible to humans but does not distract the creatures of the night, who are seemingly unaware of passers-by. Visitors are separated by natural barriers (moats, vegetation, near-invisible wires), and the lighting system resembles moonlight. Cameras are allowed but flash is prohibited. Not to be missed is the interactive **Creatures of the Night** show (daily 7.30pm, 8.30pm, 9.30pm, Fri, Sat also 10.30pm) featuring 19 species including the puma, leopard cat and spotted hyena.

ISLAND EXCURSIONS

Singapore is an island of islands. Some of its 63 nearby islets are now used for petroleum refining and storage, but a few make for excellent day trips.

Wartime memories

Singapore has a number of museums dedicated to the events of World War II. **Memories At Old Ford Factory** (351 Upper Bukit Timah Road; tel: 6462 6724; www.mof.nas.sg; Mon–Sat 9am–5.30pm, Sun noon–5.30pm) in the historic Ford factory is the site where the British surrendered to the Japanese on 15 February 1942. Nearby is **Reflections at Bukit Chandu** (31-K Pepys Road; tel: 6375 2510; www.nhb. gov.sg; Tue–Sun 9am–5.30pm), a memorial to the Malay soldiers who fought against the Japanese. On the eastern side of Singapore is the **Changi Museum** (1000 Upper Changi Road North; tel: 6214 2451; www.changimuseum.com; daily 9.30am–5pm, last admission 4.30pm; free), a small museum dedicated to prisoners of war.

Sentosa

Sentosa (tel: 1800-736 86 72; www.sentosa.com.sg), just south of the main island, is connected by the 710m (0.5-mile) Causeway Bridge. If you take a taxi directly to the drop-off point at the Resorts World casino, there is no admission fee.

A more exciting way of getting there is to take a **cable car** ride that drifts 60m (197ft) above the harbour into the heart of the island. Cable cars run continuously (8.45am to 10pm)

The Sentosa Express and Merlion statue

from Mount Faber to **HarbourFront Tower 2 and on to Sentosa Station.** Cable cars departing from The Jewel Box on Mount Faber also offer 'sky dining' (daily 6.30–8.30pm; tel: 6377 9688/6377 9633; www.mountfaber.com.sg; packages including admission fees and a guided tour of Sentosa are available).

The fastest mode of transport to the island is the light rail **Sentosa Express**. Board from the Sentosa Express station located in VivoCity shopping mall (Level 3) on the main island (first train 7am, last train midnight). The Sentosa Express stops at three stations (Waterfront, Imbiah and Beach) on Sentosa, which are within walking distance of many attractions. Otherwise, you can connect to shuttle buses and trams (free) to reach the attractions. Visitors can also get to Sentosa on foot via the Sentosa Boardwalk (daily 24 hours, ticket counter 9am–10pm, travelators 7am–midnight), parallel to Sentosa's vehicular bridge.

Sentosa served as the headquarters of the British military in the 18th century. Formerly known as Pulau Blakang Mati ('island at the back of which lies death'), the island was renamed Sentosa ('isle of peace and tranquillity') in 1972 and developed as a resort.

Sentosa's recreational opportunities are among Singapore's best. A major highlight is **Resorts World Sentosa** (www.rwsentosa.com), home to Southeast Asia's first and only **Universal Studios Singapore** ❸❽ theme park (tel: 6577 8888, daily 10am–7pm). There are seven zones and 24 themed rides, of which 18 are exclusively designed for Singapore. Highlights include Shrek's 4-Adventure, Jurassic Park Rapids Adventure, and Madagascar's tropical jungle based on the DreamWorks film, as well as the sprawling casino and several restaurants helmed by celebrity chefs such as Joel Robuchon. The resort also houses the world's largest oceanarium, **Marine Life Park** ❸❾ (www.rwsentosa.com). Within the park is the S.E.A. Aquarium, which has more than 100,000 marine animals in 49 different habitats, and over 200 sharks. At the Adventure Cove Waterpark you can snorkel with 20,000 tropical fish or float down Adventure River, passing through 14 themed zones. The Maritime Experiential Museum features an interactive voyage along the ancient Maritime Silk Route and the 360-degree multi-sensory Typhoon Theatre.

Aside from Resorts World Sentosa, most of the island's other attractions levy additional admission fees. Package tickets can be purchased online (http://store.sentosa.com.sg) or at the cable car ticketing counters at HarbourFront Tower 2 and on Mount Faber, as well as at the Beach and VivoCity Sentosa Express stations.

Many of the main attractions are grouped in a cluster named the **Imbiah Lookout**, near the Imbiah Station and the cable car station. Here the 131m (430ft) -high **Tiger Sky Tower** (www.skytower.com.sg; daily 9am–9pm) gives a bird's eye view of the Singapore skyline and the nearby southern islands. Alternatively, head up to the 37m (120ft) -high **Sentosa Merlion** statue (daily 10am–8pm).

Visitors with children may want to head to kid-friendly attractions such as the **Butterfly Park & Insect Kingdom** (www.jungle.com.sg; daily 9.30am–7pm) with over 1,500 butterflies and an exhibit of unusual insects, the interactive **Sentosa 4D Adventureland** movie theatre (tel: 6274-5355; www.4dadventureland.com.sg) first show 10am, last show 8.15pm), and the **Skyline Luge Sentosa** (daily 10am–9.30pm). Sentosa's best attraction in Imbiah Lookout is **Images of Singapore** (daily 9am–7pm), a fine wax museum housed in the colonial-style, former military hospital. This tells of Singapore's history and displays its various cultures using life-sized dioramas, artefacts, films and replicas of old street scenes.

Tiger Sky Tower

Sentosa's other historical display is **Fort Siloso Tours** (daily 10am–6pm). The original fort was built by the British in the 1880s for Singapore's defence. The interactive displays tell the fort's history from its construction through to its fall in World War II. Also here are the **Surrender Chambers**, which bring to life Singapore's formal surrender to the Japanese in 1942 with a mix of gripping audio-visual footage, artefacts and realistic wax figurines.

The **Underwater World** ⑩ (80 Siloso Road; tel: 6275 0030; www.underwaterworld.com.sg; daily 10am–7pm; charge includes that for the Dolphin Lagoon) is a small but excellent oceanarium with a submerged acrylic tunnel in its main tank. Visitors go through the tunnel on a travelator, with 2,500 sea creatures – including turtles, stingrays, sharks, sea cows and monstrous eels – overhead and on all sides. There is also a fish reflexology service (daily 10am–7pm, tel: 6279 9229) where tiny Turkish spa fish nibble away dead skin on your feet.

Underwater World also oversees the **Dolphin Lagoon** (daily 11am – 5.45pm) at Palawan Beach, where you can enjoy a show featuring Indo-Pacific Humpback Dolphins, also known as pink dolphins for their unique coloration.

Skyline Luge Sentosa

Sentosa is also popular for its beaches. The sands are soft and clean at **Palawan Beach** and **Siloso Beach**, which have good beach bars as well as sailboards, canoes and pedal boats for hire. At Siloso Beach the multimedia extravaganza **Songs of the Sea**, conceptualised by acclaimed designer Yves Pepin, dazzles audiences every evening (7.40pm and 8.40pm). Adrenalin junkies

Just one of the 1,500 butterflies at the Butterfly Park

can sign up for indoor skydiving at iFly Singapore (43 Siloso Beach Walk, next to Beach Station; tel: 6571 0000; www.ifly singapore.com).

Southern Islands

Nearby **Kusu Island** and **St John's Island** offer escapes for Singapore residents. St John's, the larger of the two, has little else besides picnicking and swimming, although its concrete promenades on the shoreline are fine for strolls. For overnight stays, a holiday bungalow is available (for bookings, tel: 1800-736 8672).

Kusu, also called Turtle Island, has more to see. Legend has it that two shipwrecked sailors – one Chinese, one Malay – were saved when a giant turtle transformed itself into an island. Each man gave thanks according to his own belief, and so today the Taoist **Tua Pek Kong Temple**, with its turtle pool, and the Muslim *keramat* (shrine) on the hill are popular places of pilgrimage. In the ninth month of the lunar calendar, usually straddling October and November, Taoists, Buddhists and Malays flock to the island. The Chinese come to pray for prosperity, good luck and fertility, while Malay pilgrims climb the 152 steps to the shrine to offer prayers.

The ferry (tel: 6534 9339; www.islandcruise.com.sg) to both islands departs Mon–Fri at 10am and 2pm, Sat at 9am, noon and 3pm, Sun and holidays at 9am, 11am, 1pm, 3pm and 5pm, from the Marina South Pier. (To get to the pier, take bus number 402 from the Marina Bay MRT Station.) The last ferry departs St John's at 2.45pm (Sat 3.45pm, Sun 5.50pm) and Kusu at 4pm (Sat 4.30pm, Sun 6.15pm).

Pulau Ubin

If time allows a visit to only one of Singapore's little islands, the best choice is **Pulau Ubin** (Granite Island), where some of the last vestiges of old Singapore cling on. Part of the fun is getting there, on a bumboat from the Changi Point Ferry Terminal (accessible by taxi or take the MRT to the Tanah Merah station, then bus number 2). The bumboat takes about 10 minutes to make the crossing. The first boat leaves Singapore at 6.30am and the last leaves Pulau Ubin at 10pm. (There is no fixed schedule; the boat departs as soon as it has 12 passengers.)

Chek Jawa

Another excellent spot to enjoy Pulau Ubin's nature offerings is Chek Jawa on the southeastern tip. The intertidal mudflats here are so fertile that they have engendered a rich ecosystem found nowhere else in Singapore. A boardwalk and a seven-storey viewing tower allow visitors to explore this unusual area. The two-hour guided tour must be booked in advance (tel: 6542 4108; daily 8.30am–6pm).

The village at the wharf on Pulau Ubin consists of a cluster of *kelong* (Malay fishing huts) and several businesses renting bicycles, which are ideal for getting around. An information kiosk (tel: 6542 4108; daily 8.30am–5pm) at the village entrance provides maps. The one-hour **Sensory Trail** guided tour is available (maximum 15 persons; bookings online at www.nparks.gov.sg). You can also follow this signposted trail on your own. You will be able to touch, see and smell fruit trees, spices and herbs used in cooking and medicine, and native plants of the

Cycling in rural Pulau Ubin

mangrove forest. The trail does not cover a large area but it rewards exploration.

Otherwise, hire a bicycle for the day. Ride past mangrove swamps, coconut palm groves, granite quarries, and rustic duck and prawn farms. Brahminy kites and white-bellied fish eagles are fairly common and easy to spot along the foreshore. Long-tailed macaques and wild boars also live here but are harder to find. Some residents still farm and fish, others serve the tourist trade and a few run seafood restaurants near the jetty.

Accommodation is available at Celestial Ubin Beach Resort (8V Pulau Ubin; tel: 6542 9749; http://ubinbeach.celestialresort.com) and overnight camping is allowed on **Mamam Beach** and the **Jelutong** campsite; no visitor's permit is required.

WHAT TO DO

Shopping and eating are the lifeblood of Singapore. Visitors will find an endless array of places to do both, economically or in high style. There is also an increasing number of venues for entertainment and sports as well as an extensive calendar of annual festivals. And no other city offers a better opportunity to introduce children to the cultures of Asia.

SHOPPING

If Singapore has a national pastime, it is shopping. Downtown is stuffed with air-conditioned malls, department stores and boutiques, and the ethnic neighbourhoods offer additional street markets and unique shops. Most shopping centres and shops are open from 10am to 9pm daily (sometimes later at weekends). Credit cards are widely accepted. Bargaining is not practised at most of the larger stores but vendors with stalls in markets often do. Many retailers can provide overseas shipping. Insist on written confirmation of your purchases and buy shipping insurance unless your credit card covers it.

Prices for many goods in Singapore are equal to or higher than those in Western countries. However, there are good discounts during the **Great Singapore Sale** (www.great singaporesale.com.sg), which runs from the last week of May through June and July.

Tax-free shopping

Although a Goods and Services Tax (GST) of 7 percent is levied on most purchases, this can be refunded if you spend a minimum of S$100 at shops participating in the Tourist

Merlion souvenirs on Sentosa

Refund Scheme (TRS). There are two central refund agencies under this scheme: **Global Blue Singapore Pte Ltd** (tel: 800 101 2813/6922 5588/421 232 111 111; www.globalblue.com) and **Premier Tax Free (Singapore) Pte Ltd** (tel: 6293 3811/1800 829 3733; www.premiertaxfree.com). Look out for shops with the 'Tax Refund' logo. Fill in a voucher for your purchases. Before your departure at Changi Airport, validate the voucher at the airport customs, then present it with your purchased items at the Global Blue counter or Premier Tax Free counter. You can opt for cash or cheque refund, or ask for the refund to be credited to your credit card or bank account.. Alternatively, file your GST claims at the eTRS (electronic tourist refund scheme; www.iras.gov.sg) self-help kiosk at Changi Airport. Look out for shops with the eTRS sign and use one credit card as a token for tagging your purchases.

Where to shop
Civic District
The **Civic District** is dominated by shopping centres and department stores. Among the biggest is **Suntec City Mall**

Money-back guarantees

Merchants at Changi Airport offer two guarantees. The first is on price. If you find you have paid more at the airport than at one of the downtown department stores and major shops on their list, they will give you a refund that is double the price difference if you can show written proof. The second guarantee is simpler. If you've bought the wrong gift or changed your mind, they will give you a full refund, no questions asked, if you return the item and receipt within 30 days. You can do this even after leaving Singapore; shipping costs will be refunded as well. For details, contact the manager of the airport shop you bought the item from, or the Civil Aviation Authority of Singapore (tel: 6542 1122; www.caas.gov.sg).

(3 Temasek Boulevard; www.
sunteccity.com.sg), filled with
mid-range food outlets as
well as plenty of fashion and
lifestyle stores. The central
circular **Fountain of Wealth**
is billed as the world's largest fountain; its waters flow
downwards instead of shoot-
ing upwards, since the traditional Chinese belief is that
water represents wealth and
the tenants here want the
water flowing directly into
their shopping centre. Other
malls and shopping arcades
in this area include **Millenia
Walk** (9 Raffles Boulevard;
www.milleniawalk.com) and
Marina Square (6 Raffles
Boulevard; www. marina
square.com.sg). **The Shoppes**

Bustling Orchard Road
is a shopping mecca

at Marina Bay Sands (10 Bayfront Avenue, www.marinabay-
sands.com) is the place to treat yourself to a luxury shopping
experience, with brands such as Chanel, Burberry, Fendi, Gucci,
Hermès and Yves Saint Laurent.

The **Raffles Hotel Shopping Arcade** (328 North Bridge
Road) has art galleries and luxury-brand boutiques. The
Raffles City Shopping Centre (252 North Bridge Road;
www.rafflescity.com.sg) nearby is linked to Suntec City Mall
by a walkway and shopping mall, appropriately dubbed the
CityLink Mall (1 Raffles Link; www.citylinkmall.com).

Other major malls include **Funan DigitaLife Mall** (109
North Bridge Road; www.funan.com.sg) and **Sim Lim**

Square (1 Rochor Canal; www.simlimsquare.com.sg), both packed with computer and electronics stores. **Bugis Junction** (200 Victoria Street; www.bugisjunction-mall.com.sg) is a glass-covered mall that retains its shophouse architecture; across the street from it is the **Bugis Street market**.

Bugis + (201 Victoria Street; www.bugis-plus.com.sg) is linked via a bridge to Bugis Junction at Level 2. Mid-range stores and fashion boutiques are targeted at a younger crowd. There is a cineplex on the fifth level.

Orchard Road

Orchard Road is another major downtown shopping strip, renowned for its upscale international stores. **ION Orchard** (2 Orchard Turn; www.ionorchard.com) is the most exciting of the recent additions here, with over 300 retail, F&B and entertainment stores. **313@Somerset** (313 Orchard Road; www.313somerset.com.sg) sits above the Somerset MRT station and caters to shoppers' passions for fashion and food. There's a huge Food Republic food court on the fifth level. Next door is **Orchard Gateway**, Orchard Road's newest shopping centre which is made up of two buildings on diagonally opposite sites, linked via a glass bridge. Among its 50 or so tenants are American lifestyle store Crate & Barrel and the library@orchard public library. A stone's throw away is **Orchard Central** (181 Orchard Road; www.orchardcentral.com.sg) filled with independent retail stores and eateries including Dean & Deluca from New York. **Knightsbridge** (270 Orchard Road; www.knightsbridge.com.sg) houses the largest Topshop/Topman outlet outside the UK and the US and the popular Abercrombie and Fitch store.

Among the favourites of the older shopping malls are **Wisma Atria** (435 Orchard Road; www.wismaonline.com), noted for its fashion boutiques and Food Republic food court; **Ngee Ann City** (391 Orchard Road; www.

ngeeanncity.com.sg), with the Japanese department store Takashimaya and Kinokuniya bookstore; **Paragon** (290 Orchard Road; www.paragon.com.sg), with numerous luxury boutiques, and **Centrepoint** (176 Orchard Road; www.centrepoint.com.sg), long a favourite of Singaporeans. **Far East Plaza** (14 Scotts Road) has trendy streetwear at low prices. Two popular home-grown emporiums are **Tangs** (320 Orchard Road; www.tangs.com) with well-loved fashion, beauty and household sections, and **Robinsons** (260 Orchard Road; www.robinsons.com.sg), Singapore's oldest department store with a 155-year history.

DFS Galleria (25 Scotts Road; www.dfsgalleria.com) is a treasure trove of designer fashion and cosmetics with duty-free savings. Slightly further away **Tanglin Shopping Centre** (19 Tanglin Road; www.tanglinsc.com) has the city's largest selection of Persian rugs, old maps and Asian antiques.

Henna tattooist in Little India

Little India fabric vendor

Chinatown

Singapore's ethnic neighbourhoods offer more unusual shopping possibilities. Chinatown is headlined by **Yue Hwa Emporium** (70 Eu Tong Sen Street; tel: 6538 4222; www.yuehwa.com.sg), a department store where all the clothing, household goods and crafts are from Taiwan and China. **People's Park Centre** (101 Upper Cross Street) is filled with Chinese vendors willing to bargain while **People's Park Complex** (1 Park Road) has fabrics and streetwear.

Little India

Little India is the area to poke around for bangles, gold jewellery, silk saris and Indian spices. **Little India Arcade** on 48 Serangoon Road has over 50 small shops and the nearby **Tekka Centre** (665 Buffalo Road) has a wet market and scores of shops selling saris, batiks and brassware. **Mustafa Centre** (145 Syed Alwi Road; tel: 6295 5855; www.mustafa.com.sg) is a large 24-hour department store popular for its low-priced electronic goods, groceries and garments.

Suburbs

VivoCity (1 HarbourFront Walk; www.vivocity.com.sg), a shopping and entertainment centre with the largest retail venue in Singapore features cineplexes, a hypermarket and

Jamie's Italian, celebrity chef Jamie Oliver's first restaurant in Asia.

Suburban malls offer many of the same goods available downtown, but often at much better prices. **Century Square** (2 Tampines Central 5; www.centurysquare.com.sg) is beside the Tampines MRT Station; **Junction 8** (9 Bishan Place; www.junction8.com.sg) is served by the Bishan MRT Station, and **JEM** (50 Jurong Gateway Road; www.jem.sg) and **Westgate** (3 Gateway Drive, www.westgate.com.sg) are located next to Jurong East MRT Station.

Specialist shops
Antiques and handicrafts
There is a cluster of antique shops at **Tanglin Shopping Centre** (19 Tanglin Road); if you purchase something there, request shipping and certificates of authenticity. Stores include **Lopburi Arts & Antiques** (01-20; tel: 6738 3834); **Antiques of the Orient** (02-40; tel: 6734 9351; www.aoto.com.sg), **Akemi Gallery** (02-06; tel: 6735 6315; www.akemigallery.com), and **Hassan's Carpets** (03-01/06; tel: 6737 56 26; www.hassanscarpets.com). **Dempsey Road** (Tanglin Village), near the Botanic Gardens, is also filled with many tiny antique and Asian collectible shops, such as **Asia Passion** (Block 13, 01-02;

Complaints departments

Singapore has several means to rectify retailer malfeasance. You can lodge complaints with the Singapore Tourism Board by calling its hotline 1800-736 2000 (toll-free in Singapore) or going online at www.yoursingapore.com. Alternatively, contact the Small Claims Tribunal (1st level, Subordinate Courts, 1 Havelock Square; tel: 6435 5946; www.small claims.gov.sg). At the latter, complaints are heard on short notice and judgements are rendered on the spot.

tel: 6473 1339) and **Woody Antique House** (Block 13, 01-05; tel: 6471 1770). **Kwok Gallery** (03-01 Far East Shopping Centre, 545 Orchard Road; tel: 6235 2516) has dealt in genuine Chinese pieces since 1918.

Bookstores

Singapore's leading bookstores are **Kinokuniya** (03-09/10/15 Ngee Ann City, 391 Orchard Road; tel: 6737 5021; 03-50 Liang Court, 177 River Valley Road, tel: 6337 1300; 03-09/12 Bugis Junction, 200 Victoria Street; tel: 6339 1790; 04-23 JEM, 50 Jurong Gateway Road; tel: 6430 0868; www.kinokuniya.com. sg) and **Times Bookstores** (04-08 Centrepoint, 176 Orchard Road; tel: 6734 9022; 04-41 Paragon, 290 Orchard Road; tel: 6836 6182; www.timesbookstores.com.sg). The small, independent **Select Books** (03-15 Tanglin Shopping Centre, 19 Tanglin Road; tel: 6732 1515; www.selectbooks.com.sg) has a rich collection of Singapore and Southeast Asian books.

Tailors

CYC The Custom Shop (02-12 Raffles Hotel Arcade, 328 North Bridge Road; tel: 6336 3556; www.cyccustom-shop.com), established in 1935, was the first company in Singapore to offer custom-made shirts. Fabrics from Italy, Switzerland, France and Japan are used for the fine quality shirts. **Coloc Tailor** (02-29 Raffles Hotel Arcade, 328 North Bridge Road; tel: 6338 9767; www.coloc.com.sg) can complete a suit in 24 hours. **Pimab's** (32B Boat Quay; tel: 6538 6466; www.pimabs.com), helmed by local fashion designer Leslie Chia, specialises in bespoke services for men at reasonable prices. Far East Plaza at 14 Scotts Road also has tailors

Quality control

Shops displaying the CaseTrust (CT) logo are accredited as reliable and honest by the Consumers Association of Singapore.

that offer made-to-measure clothes. **Solito** (02-95; tel: 6732 8468) and **Ascott Tailors** (02-88; tel: 6734 2207) can have your clothes ready within eight hours.

ENTERTAINMENT

In addition to its shopping, eating and cultural attractions, Singapore has a thriving nightlife scene, although it remains a tamer one than those found in some other Asian and Western capitals.

Performing arts

Singapore's impresarios bring in performances by international groups and

Chinese opera performers

artists. Current attractions are listed in tourist magazines such as *Where Singapore* and in the dailies. Tickets can be purchased at sistic (tel: 6348 5555) box offices; bookings can also be made at www.sistic.com.sg. The **Singapore Arts Festival** (www.sifa.sg) held in August and September, is well regarded for its line-up of innovative works. The **Singapore Night Festival** (www.brasbasahbugis.sg), a nocturnal festival held over two weekends in August, showcases spectacular aerial performances, music and dance performances, and installation artworks at various museums in the Bras Basah district.

The **Fort Canning Centre** hosts outdoor performances such as rock concerts and ballets. Singapore has some Chinese opera companies, which often perform on outdoor stages in Chinatown and at annual festivals, particularly during the Festival of the Hungry Ghosts around August. The **Chinese Opera Teahouse** (5 Smith Street; tel: 6323 4862; www. ctcopera.com) offers performances of opera excerpts with English subtitles (showtimes Fri and Sat 7–9pm; admission fee inclusive of set dinner).

The iconic **Esplanade – Theatres on the Bay** (1 Esplanade Drive; tel: 6828 8377; www.esplanade.com) is Singapore's world-class performing arts centre. Music, theatre, dance and outdoor performances are hosted in this large complex. The noted **Singapore Symphony Orchestra** performs here regularly; check www.sso.org.sg for programme updates. The 10-day **Mosaic Music Festival**, which celebrates world music, is also held here in March every year.

The Marina Bay Sands integrated resort includes **The Sands Theater** and **The Grand Theater** (10 Bayfront Avenue; tel: 6688 8868; www.marinabaysands.com), with stunning interior design and sophisticated technology. Major musicals such as *The Lion King and Wicked* are shown here.

NIGHTLIFE

With hundreds of clubs, bars, and karaoke lounges, late-night entertainment options are plenty. Some places have dress codes so check with the venue beforehand if you're unsure.

Singapore River

For those seeking a leisurely drink, Singapore has a large number of chic bars and lounges, many with outdoor seating. The **Boat Quay** shophouses are home to a few such establishments. **Harry's Bar** (28 Boat Quay; tel: 6538 3029; www. harrys.com.sg) offers live jazz. **Molly Malone's Irish Pub** (56

Head to Boat Quay for chic bars and lounges

Circular Road; tel: 6536 2029; www.molly-malone.com) and the Victorian **Penny Black** (26–27 Boat Quay; tel: 6538 2300; www.pennyblack.com.sg) are excellent places to down pints of Guinness. Just across the river is **Bar Opiume** (1 Empress Place Waterfront; tel: 6339 2876), a sophisticated chill-out place stylish to the core.

Clarke Quay (tel: 6337 3292; www.clarkequay.com.sg) has hip restaurants, bars and dance clubs like **Attica** (01-03, 3A River Valley; tel: 6333 9973; www.attica.com.sg).

The top club **Zouk** (17 Jiak Kim Street; tel: 6738 2988; www.zoukclub.com) is unmissable. Ever the trendsetter, it features a wine bar, three clubs and international DJs.

Civic District

Paulaner Bräuhaus (01-01 Millenia Walk, 9 Raffles Boulevard; tel: 6883 2572; www.paulaner-brauhaus.com/singapore), is a popular German microbrewery serving delicious Bavarian bites and entertainment especially during Oktoberfest.

At the **Long Bar** (Raffles Hotel, 1 Beach Road; tel: 6337 1886), Singapore Slings are must-haves, and the vertigo-inducing **New Asia Bar** at Swissôtel The Stamford (71st & 72nd Floors, 2 Stamford Road; tel: 6837 3322) offers fabulous city views. **Anti:dote** at the lobby level of Fairmont Singapore (80 Bras Basah Road; tel: 6431 5315; www.fairmont.com/singapore) is a cocktail bar that has received rave reviews for its experimental concoctions and modern tapas.

The Butter Factory (1 Fullerton Road; tel: 6423 9804; www.thebutterfactory.com) is where the beautiful people hang out and a popular spot on top of the Marina Bay Sands Hotel is **Ku De Ta** (Marina Bay Sands North Tower, 1 Bayfront Avenue; tel: 6688 7688; www.kudeta.com.sg). **Pangaea** (B2-05 Crystal Pavilion South, Marina Bay Sands, 10 Bayfront Ave; tel:

New Asia Bar at Swissôtel The Stamford

6688-7448; www.pangaea.sg) is an exclusive club which can be
reached via an underwater tunnel connected to The Shoppes
at Marina Bay Sands. Resident and international DJs entertain
party-goers at this Ultra-Lounge founded by Michael Ault.

Orchard Road

On **Emerald Hill** beside the Centrepoint Shopping Centre
are several hot spots. The Spanish-inspired wine bar **Que Pasa**
(7 Emerald Hill Road; tel: 6235 6626) presents sangria and
tapas while **Ice Cold Beer** (9 Emerald Hill Road; tel: 6735
9929) serves beer straight from the tanks. At the western end
of Orchard Road are **Brix** (Basement One, Grand Wing, Grand
Hyatt, 10 Scotts Road; tel: 6732 1234), with beautiful people
and special theme nights, and the ever popular **Hard Rock
Café** (02-01 hpl House, 50 Cuscaden Road; tel: 6235 5232;
www.hardrock.com) with live music. All have cover charges
that usually include one or two drinks. There's also the stylish
Balaclava Live (05-02 ION Orchard, 2 Orchard Turn; tel: 6634
8377; www.imaginings.com.sg), which has a resident band.

Sentosa

Sentosa Island has a few laid-back beach bars, great for sunset
drinks. The stylish **Tanjong Beach Club** (120 Tanjong Beach
Walk; tel: 6270 1355; www.tanjongbeachclub.com) is an all-
day beach hideout offering excellent food and cocktails. Sip
cocktails on a deck chair at **Coastes** (50 Siloso Beach Walk;
tel: 6631 8938; www.coastes.com) or pick up a surfboard
and ride artificial waves and enjoy live music and modern
Californian-Asian cuisine at **Wave House Sentosa** (Siloso
Beach; tel: 6377 3113; www.wavehousesentosa.com).

Across Sentosa and next to VivoCity is **St James Power
Station** (3 Sentosa Gateway; tel: 6270 7676; www.stjames
powerstation.com), which offers several bars and live music
venues under one roof.

SPORTS

Singapore has good facilities for sports activities. Active visitors should take heed of the high humidity and schedule outdoor workouts for early mornings or evenings.

Biking. Rentals are available at Sentosa, East Coast Park, Pasir Ris Park and Pulau Ubin.

Sea sports. Kayaking is available at Sentosa, East Coast Park and Changi Point while **cable skiing** is found at East Coast Lagoon (1206A, East Coast Parkway; tel: 6442 7318; www.ski360degree.com). **Waterskiing** and **wakeboarding** are available at the Kallang River. **Windsurfing, sailing and kitesurfing** equipment and can be rented from **Constant Wind** (11 Changi Coast Walk; tel: 6445 5108; www.constantwind.com), a seasports and sailing school.

Golf. Several of Singapore's golf courses are world class, attracting such international tournaments as the Johnnie Walker Classic. There are 11 private golf courses offering limited access to non-members and four public courses that have no restrictions on visitors. Green fees range from S$40 for a nine-hole course on weekdays to S$400 for a full round at a championship course on weekends. Some clubs may ask you for a proficiency certificate. Clubs include **Changi Golf Club** (20 Netheravon Road; tel: 6545 5133; www.changigolfclub.org.sg) with a nine-hole course and sea views; **Orchid Country Club** (1 Orchid Club Road; tel: 6750 2111/6755 9811; www.orchidclub.com), which offers night golfing; the **Singapore Island Country Club** (180 Island Club Road; tel: 6459 2222; www.sicc.org.sg) with four 18-hole courses amidst the verdant MacRitchie Reservoir; **Sentosa Golf Club** (27 Bukit Manis Road, Sentosa Island; tel: 6275 0090; www.sentosagolf.com) with two beautiful championship 18-hole courses, and **Tanah Merah Country Club** (25 Changi Coast Road; tel: 6542 3040; www.tmcc.org.sg), also with two 18-hole courses.

Sungei Buloh Wetland Reserve

Hiking. Despite the heat and humidity, hiking is one of Singapore's most attractive outdoor pursuits. The **Bukit Timah Nature Reserve** (177 Hindhede Drive; tel: 6468 5736/1800 471 7300; www.nparks.gov.sg), **Sungei Buloh Wetland Reserve** (301 Neo Tiew Crescent; www.sbwr.org.sg) and **MacRitchie Nature Trail** (off Thomson Road at the Central Catchment Nature Reserve) are the three most popular trekking areas.

Spectator sports. Among the most popular are **cricket** and **rugby**, matches of which you might see at the Padang across from City Hall. The annual SCC International Rugby Sevens tournament is held here. Singapore also has its own **soccer** league (www.sleague.com), in which local and international teams compete at stadiums around the island. The **F1 Singapore Grand Prix** in September (tel: 6738 6738; www.singaporegp.sg) was the first night race in F1 history.

Horseracing. Races can be enjoyed at the Singapore Turf Club (1 Turf Club Avenue, beside the Kranji MRT Station;

Singapore is home to many theme parks

tel: 6879 1000; www.turfclub. com.sg) on selected Friday nights and Saturday and Sunday afternoons.

SINGAPORE FOR CHILDREN

Singapore has many attractions and entertainment options designed for visitors of all ages, most offering child discounts. With its beaches, oceanarium and theme parks, **Sentosa** (see page 73) is practically made for children. One of the best attractions is **Universal Studios Singapore** (8 Sentosa Gateway; www.rwsentosa.com) housed in the Resorts World Sentosa integrated resort. Other attractions include a Marine Life Park and Maritime Xperiential Museum.

The **zoo** (see page 69) has a special area for younger children, and the **Night Safari** (see page 71) provides something exciting for families after nightfall. The River Safari (see page 71). home to the Giant pandas from China, is a must-visit. The **Jurong BirdPark** (see page 66), whose inhabitants range from hornbills to pelicans, has highly entertaining shows.

The **Haw Par Villa** (see page 65) gives kids a chance to experience Chinese culture. The **Singapore Discovery Centre** (510 Upper Jurong Road; tel: 6792 6188; www.sdc.com.sg) is a high-tech 'edutainment' attraction celebrating the history of Singapore. The **Singapore Science Centre** (15 Science Centre Road; tel: 6425 2500; www.science.edu.sg) has over 850 exhibits, an aviation gallery and an Omni-theatre. Nearby is **Snow City** (21 Jurong Town Hall Road; tel: 6560 2306; www.snowcity. com. sg), where there is skiing and snowboarding indoors year-round.

Calendar of events

Check exact dates of these major festivals and events with the Singapore Tourism Board (tel: 1800-736 2000; www.yoursingapore.com).

January/February *Chinese New Year:* lion dances, night bazaar and festival in Chinatown; *Chingay:* Orchard Road street parade with floats and stilt-walkers; *Thaipusam:* Hindu devotees carry metal structures *(kavadi)* on a 3km (2-mile) pilgrimage of penance from Little India's Sri Srinivasa Perumal Temple to Sri Thandayuthapani (Chettiar) Temple in Tank Road.

March/April *World Gourmet Summit:* restaurants host international celebrity chefs. *Mosaic Music Festival* held at Esplanade.

May/June/July *Vesak Day:* birds released at temples to mark Buddha's entrance into Nirvana; *Singapore Dragon Boat Festival:* Chinese eat glutinous rice dumplings and join in dragon boat races to honour Qu Yuan, a patriotic martyr; *Great Singapore Sale:* huge discounts for eight weeks; *Singapore Food Festival:* an annual gourmet splash in July.

August/September *Hungry Ghosts Festival:* spirits of the dead return in the 7th lunar month, with street banquets and Chinese operas; *National Day:* celebrates independence with a massive parade and fireworks; *F1 Singapore Grand Prix:* premier racing event; *Mooncake (Lantern) Festival:* traditional mid-autumn festivities in Chinatown and Chinese Garden. *Singapore Arts Festival:* the best performing arts from the East and West.

October/November/December *Navarathiri Festival:* nine nights devoted to three Hindu goddesses, with music and procession at Sri Mariamman Temple; *Deepavali:* the Festival of Lights is celebrated in homes, Hindu temples and in the streets of Little India; *Thimithi Festival:* devotees walk over burning coals at the Sri Mariamman Temple; *Festival Light-Ups:* in Little India (Deepavali), Orchard Road (Christmas) and Geylang Serai (Hari Raya); *ZoukOut Dance Party:* international DJs spin from dusk to dawn.

Variable *Hari Raya Puasa:* Muslims celebrate the end of Ramadan (fasting month) with prayers, feasts and home visits; *Hari Raya Haji:* marks the sacrifices made by Muslims who undertake the *haj* (pilgrimage to Mecca)

EATING OUT

Singapore is one of the world's premier dining destinations with over 20,000 restaurants, cafés and food courts. This small country is situated (geographically, historically and ethnically) on a culinary axis point where several of the world's top cuisines mingle, from the great regional traditions of Chinese and Indian cooking to the more localised Malay and the Peranakan (Straits Chinese) cuisines. Thai, Indonesian, Japanese and Korean food is also amply represented, as is first-rate fare from the West. Eating out is also convenient, with good service and hygiene and English spoken. Meals in hawker centres are particularly affordable and of excellent value.

Be sure to sample each of Singapore's celebrated cuisines. Try out the various settings too, from hawker centres and independent cafés to top hotel restaurants. Ask locals for tips, check out the latest local listings in the dailies and online food portals such as www.soshiok.com. Or download the 8 DAYS Eat app for a huge range of recommendations.

For dinner, especially on weekends, reservations are a must at establishments that accept them. Otherwise, join the lines at the various eateries. It is nearly always worth the wait.

Hawker centres and food courts

Hawker centres are Singapore's answer to fast-food restaurants. Meals are very cheap, with main courses costing just a few dollars. Pictures of each dish often decorate a food hawker's counter, accompanied by names in English. Most offer a variety of freshly cooked Chinese, Malay and Indian choices. Your food is sometimes brought to your table; other times you pick up your order on a tray. Singapore's most popular hawker centres are **Maxwell Food Centre** near Chinatown, **Newton**

Maxwell Food hawker centre

Circus across the Newton MRT Station and **Lau Pa Sat** near the Raffles Place MRT Station.

   Food courts are slightly fancier than hawker centres, often located in shopping malls. These are air-conditioned, and prices are generally higher, but the same procedures apply.

Chinese cuisine

The majority of Singaporeans are ethnically Chinese, so regional Chinese cuisines are amply represented. From Cantonese dim sum and Peking duck to Teochew rice porridge and Sichuan *mala* (spicy) hot pot steamboat, the choices offered by Chinese restaurants are endless.

   Street-food-style offerings from Chinese hawkers are must tries. Popular dishes include *char kway teow* (fried rice noodles with clams, Chinese sausage and egg tossed with soy sauce), *popiah* (spring rolls with various fillings), *wonton mee* (egg noodles topped with minced meat or shrimp dumplings and sliced roast pork) and *yong tau foo* (beancurd stuffed with meat). Undoubtedly the single most popular dish is Hainanese chicken rice (poached chicken served with fragrant rice cooked in chicken stock and accompanied by a piquant chilli-ginger sauce). This is a staple at hawker centres, food courts and most Chinese coffee shops.

Malay cuisine

Malay dishes tend to be spicy, livened up with ingredients such as lemongrass, chillies, cloves, tamarind and shrimp paste *(belacan)*. Coconut milk is also often added to temper the spiciness. For religious reasons, pork is never used.

A popular dish is *satay*, skewers of meat that are spiced and marinated before barbecuing. Satay, usually beef, mutton and chicken, is often accompanied by *ketupat* (steamed rice wrapped in coconut leaves), cucumber, onions and a spicy peanut sauce.

Among other savoury Malay offerings are *mee rebus* (yellow noodles in a thick spicy gravy), *gado gado* (vegetable salad smothered in a coconut and peanut sauce, served with prawn crackers), *nasi goreng* (Malay-style fried rice), *soto ayam* (spicy chicken soup with rice cakes) *rendang* (beef slowly cooked in coconut milk and spices) and curries.

Peranakan (Nyonya) cuisine

Nyonya (which refers to the women of a Peranakan or Straits-Chinese family of mixed Chinese and Malay heritage) cuisine is Singapore's most indigenous. Chinese and Malay ingredients and recipes have been transformed into some of Singapore's most delicious dishes. There are a few Peranakan restaurants in Katong in the eastern part of Singapore.

Coconut milk, shrimp paste *(belacan)* and chillies give Nyonya dishes a unique flavour. Shrimp paste, chilli and lime are pounded together to form a condiment called *sambal belacan*. Dishes worth trying are *buah keluak* (chicken and black nuts in tamarind sauce), *laksa* (rice noodles in curry sauce), *nyonya kueh* (glutinous rice cakes usually made with coconut milk and palm sugar) and *otak-otak* (minced fish flavoured with lime and coconut, wrapped in banana leaves and charcoal roasted).

Indian cuisine
The Indian food in Singapore is on a par with the best dishes in India. Diners are treated to the best of northern

Crsipy fried prawns

Chilli crab

and southern Indian dishes, as well as creations that are uniquely Singaporean.

Northern Indian cuisine is mild and subtle, often employing yoghurt, wheat breads and ghee (clarified butter) rather than cooking oils. Tandoori (marinated meat or fish cooked in clay ovens) is the signature dish. In Singapore, the local variations on traditional northern Indian recipes have produced dishes like *mee goreng* (bean curd, mutton and peas fried with thick noodles in a tomato sauce) and *sup kambing* (a mutton soup accompanied by French bread).

Southern Indian cuisine is spicier and often less pricey. This is most often served in 'banana-leaf' restaurants, where a banana leaf replaces the plate. Rice is ladled onto the big leaf, followed by mounds of chutneys, dal (pureed lentils) and curries. The meal is eaten by hand, with the rice pinched between one's fingers. Vegetarians will enjoy southern Indian food as many dishes are meatless. Little India has a number of inexpensive vegetarian restaurants. Muslim Indian restaurants avoid pork but use other meats, especially in dishes such as *biryani*, which has a basmati-rice base.

Indian cooking is known for its breads, ranging from the unleavened *chapati* to the fluffy *puri*. In Singapore, a popular bread is *roti prata*, a large, thin, folded pancake cooked on a griddle. When filled with spicy mutton (or chicken) and egg, it becomes *murtabak*, a staple at Indian street stalls and hawker centres.

Strangely enough, the best-known Indian dish in Singapore is not Indian at all, but rather a regional invention, the fish-head curry. The fish head is usually that of a red snapper, boiled in a spicy curry and served eyeball-up.

Seafood

The seafood restaurants along East Coast Parkway, facing the sea, do brisk business nearly every night. What's served is simply the fresh catch of the day, often perfectly prepared in any style you wish, with sauces of your choice. You can have squid deep fried, prawns in garlic and stingrays barbecued. Singapore's most popular signature seafood is chilli crab; pepper crab comes a close second. These are whole crabs stir fried with a fiery chilli or black pepper sauce.

Eurasian food

Eurasian cuisine comprises flavours from Singapore's minority community of Portuguese, Dutch, Malay, Javanese and Indian ancestry. A typical dish is devil curry (chicken perked up with vinegar, mustard and chillies). Other specialties with a Western

Tea with the Queen

The perfect shopping and sightseeing break in bustling Singapore is a visit to a traditional Chinese teahouse. Singapore's best known is **Tea Chapter** (9/11 Neil Road; tel: 6226 1175; http://teachapter.com), located near Jinriksha Station. On 10 October 1989, Queen Elizabeth II and Prince Philip took their tea here in a private room upstairs overlooking the street. Visitors today can appreciate the pleasures of Chinese tea culture in the same room. The teas run the gamut, from greens to reds, but the service is traditional. Water is heated at the table, the tea arrives in tiny packets, and scoops, tea clips, fragrance cups, saucers and snacks complete the graceful setting.

touch include stews and roasts, usually enhanced with the addition of soy sauce, green chillies or sour tamarind juice. The Eurasian family's Christmas table is always laden with these dishes, including a traditional item called *feng* – a type of curry made of pork and offal.

European cuisines

French, Italian, Spanish, and Mediterranean restaurants are scattered across Singapore. Top Western restaurants with foreign chefs are a staple in Singapore's international hotels, and finding a French restaurant with a French chef at the helm is easy.

In Singapore's high-end restaurants, you can find innovative, modern European cuisine using the freshest seasonal ingredients. Although there is no Michelin Guide in Singapore, this city has attracted many Michelin-starred chefs to set up shop here. Boosting Singapore's reputation as a gastronomic city are restaurants by celebrity chefs from Tokyo, Paris, Sydney and New York, the majority of them located at Marina Bay Sands and Resorts World Sentosa.

Cookery schools

Several culinary schools offer introductory courses to Asian cuisine, lasting from a day to several weeks. **The Coriander Leaf** restaurant (3A Merchant Court, 02-03 River Valley Road, Clarke Quay; tel. 6732 3354; www.corianderleaf.com) teaches the preparation of Southeast Asian, Middle Eastern and fusion cuisines. **Shermay's Cooking School** (Block 43 Jalan Merah Saga, 01-76 Chip Bee Gardens, Holland Village; tel: 6479 8442; www.shermay.com) introduces Nyonya cooking as well as Western cuisine and pastry classes. **Sam.leong@forest cooking school** (Forest Restaurant, Equarius Hotel, 8 Sentosa Gateway; tel: 9672 4221; www.samatforest.com), helmed by renowned Chinese chef Sam Leong, teaches foodies how to make Chinese food.

Exotic fruits

Singapore's fresh-produce markets are the places to find vegetables and fruits not normally seen in Western supermarkets. The most notorious is the durian, known as the king of fruits and well loved by most Singaporeans. This spiny delight fetches royal prices, but to most foreigners, its smell is well beyond polite description. Public buildings and MRT stations display signs prohibiting the durian's very presence.

Singapore's succulent, but infamous, durian fruit

Among fruits commonly found in Singapore are the rambutan (red and hairy in appearance), mangosteen (purple outside, white inside), *chiku* (brownish), starfruit (aptly named after its shape) and the red-and-white 'dragon fruit', whose mild taste is neither smoky nor fiery but similar to that of kiwi fruit.

Drinks

Ginger tea (*teh halia*), a staple of Indian drink vendors, is a strong contender to the lattes of Starbucks and other coffee chains. An even more direct contender is *kopi tarik*, the 'pulled coffee' that is 'pulled' by the maker from cup to pitcher and back again to ensure the ingredients are well mixed. Little India abounds with 'pulled-coffee' stalls. The same stunt is used to produce *teh tarik*, noted for its delicious froth.

In hawker centres and food courts, try freshly squeezed juices, or a cold glass of soya bean milk or sugar cane juice with a wedge of lemon. The local beer is Tiger, a refreshing pilsner-style beer. Chinese teas are favoured by many Singaporean Chinese, served hot.

PLACES TO EAT

We have used the following symbols to give an idea of the price for a three-course meal for one, including wine, cover and service:

$$$$	over $60	**$$**	$20–40
$$$	$40–60	**$**	under $20

SINGAPORE RIVER

Absinthe $$$$ *71/72 Boat Quay; tel: 6222 9068; www.absinthe. sg.* Open Monday to Friday for lunch, daily for dinner. This restaurant overlooking the river is an ideal spot for an elegant French meal. Chef Francois Mermilliod expertly prepares dishes such as pan-fried foie gras with morello cherries and lobster bisque scented with cognac. Match your meal with fine French wines.

Brewerkz $$$ *01-05/06 Riverside Point, 30 Merchant Road; tel: 6438 7438; www.brewerkz.com.* Open daily for lunch and dinner. Handcrafted beer fresh from its on-site microbrewery and hearty American cuisine in an industrial-like setting. It offers six signature beers, including the bestselling Golden Ale, as well as seven seasonal beers.

Glutton's Bay $ *01-15 Esplanade Mall; tel: 6438 4038.* Open daily for dinner and supper. Dine on some of Singapore's best-loved street food under the moonlight. A popular spot with both locals and tourists, Glutton's Bay has 12 push-cart hawkers selling favourites like barbecued chicken wings, *char kway teow* (fried flat noodles with clams in dark sauce) and oyster omelette.

Jade $$$ *The Fullerton Hotel, 1 Fullerton Square; tel: 6877 8188; www.fullertonhotel.com.* Open daily for lunch and dinner. Jade serves up a sophisticated menu of Cantonese classics amid grand surroundings. The weekend a la carte dim sum buffet lunch serves exquisite creations such as deep-fried taro paste with truffle and mushroom.

The Lighthouse $$$$ *Level 8, The Fullerton Hotel, 1 Fullerton Square; tel: 6877 8933; www.fullertonhotel.com.* Open Monday to Friday for lunch, daily for dinner. This small restaurant presents a fabulous fine dining Italian experience with stunning views. A great venue for romantic nights or special occasions. Well executed dishes include beef carpaccio and homemade *tagliolini* with Amalfi's lemon sauce and spiced prawns.

Waku Ghin $$$$ *1 Marina Bay Sands, 10 Bayfront Avenue, Level 2 Casino; tel: 6688 8504; www.wakughin.com.* Open Tuesday to Sunday for dinner (two seatings). Tetsuya Wakuda's first restaurant outside Sydney is one of the high profile celebrity chef establishments at Marina Bay Sands. Enjoy the chef's highly acclaimed European cuisine with Japanese influence, prepared with the freshest seasonal ingredients. The wines and bay views are just as sublime.

CIVIC DISTRICT

Equinox $$$–$$$$ *68–72 Floors, Swissôtel The Stamford, 2 Stamford Road; tel: 6431 5669.* Open daily for lunch and dinner. A complex of five restaurants and bars sits atop the hotel. Start with drinks at the New Asia Bar on the 71st level while taking in stunning city views through its floor-to-ceiling windows, then descend one level to swanky restaurant Jaan which continues to receive rave reviews for its seasonal degustation menus.

Lei Garden $$$ *01-24 Chijmes, 30 Victoria Street; tel: 6339 3822.* Open daily for lunch and dinner. One of Singapore's best Cantonese restaurants, Lei Garden is renowned for its *dim sum* lunches and fresh seafood dishes (shark, abalone, lobster) served in an exquisite formal setting.

Mikuni $$$$ *Level 3, Fairmont Singapore, 80 Bras Basah Road; tel: 6431 6156. www.fairmont.com/singapore/dining/mikuni.* Open daily for lunch and dinner. Choose to sit at the *teppanyaki*, sushi or *robatayaki* counters where you can watch the chefs in action. Otherwise, opt for the main dining area where you can feast on the highly creative *kaiseki* menu featuring the best seasonal produce. The lunch bento sets are just as exquisite.

True Blue $$$ *47/49 Armenian Street; tel: 6440 4548;* www.true bluecuisine.com. Open Tuesday to Saturday for lunch and dinner. Just two doors away from the Peranakan Museum, this eatery is adorned with the owner Benjamin Seck's personal collection of Peranakan antiques and artefacts. Try favourites like spicy beef *rendang* and *ayam buah keluak* (chicken stewed with Indonesian black nuts).

CHINATOWN AND CBD

Bar-Roque Grill $$$$ *01-00, 165 Tanjong Pagar Road; tel: 6444 9672;* www.bar-roque.com.sg. Open Tuesday to Friday and Sunday for lunch and dinner, Saturday for dinner. Alsace-born Chef Stephane Istel, formerly of DB Bistro Moderne, serves large platters of food designed for sharing. The massive rotisserie churns out all kinds of delicious meats such as juicy free-range chicken and pork-knuckle. The Butchers' Sunday menu is incredibly popular.

Majestic Restaurant $$$$ *1/F, New Majestic Hotel, 31–37 Bukit Pasoh Road; tel: 6511 4718;* www.restaurantmajestic. com. Open daily for lunch and dinner. This stylish restaurant is known for its individually-plated, modern Cantonese cuisine such as grilled rack of lamb in Chinese honey sauce and braised lobster in a creamy milk and lime sauce. Diners get a view of swimmers in the pool above through port holes in the ceiling.

Maxwell Food Centre $ *Maxwell Road, next to the URA Centre.* Open daily from breakfast until supper. Join any of the long queues at one of Singapore's oldest food centres. Try the fish noodles, chicken rice or porridge and other local delights. Avoid weekday lunch hours when executives arrive in droves from the nearby CBD offices.

Spring Court $$$ *52-56 Upper Cross Street; tel: 6449 5030;* www. springcourt.com.sg. Open daily for lunch and dinner. This successful family-run restaurant, established in 1929, is considered one of the oldest Cantonese restaurants in Singapore. Make your way to this four-storey heritage building in Chinatown and enjoy classics such as crisp roast chicken and golden cereal prawns. *Dim sum* is available for lunch.

LITTLE INDIA AND KAMPING GLAM

Banana Leaf Apolo $$ *54 Race Course Road, Little India; tel: 6293 8682; www.bananaleafapolo.com.* Open daily lunch and dinner. Within walking distance of Little India MRT station, this is one of the city's most popular South Indian restaurants, famed for its fiery fish-head curry. Meals are served on banana leaves. There is a second outlet at Little India Arcade (01-32, 48 Serangoon Road; tel: 6297 1595).

Hajjah Maimunah $ *11–15 Jalan Pisang, Kampong Glam; tel: 6297 4294; www.hjmaimunah.com.* Open Monday to Saturday for breakfast, lunch and dinner. This no-frills eatery, which serves some of the best Malay food in town, is always packed. Just point to the dishes behind the glass counter and indicate how many of you are eating. The tender beef *rendang* curry just melts in your mouth, and the *sotong bakar* (grilled squid) is exceptional. No credit cards.

Komala Vilas $ *76–78 Serangoon Road, Little India; tel: 6293 6980; www.komalavilas.com.sg.* Open daily. Singapore's classic southern Indian vegetarian restaurant (six decades old) provides an unforgettable dining experience. Recommended are its spicy rice and lentil curries served on banana leaf, chutneys and *thosais* (vegetable-stuffed crêpes). Eat with your hands – there are washbasins on the wall. There is another outlet nearby at 12–14 Buffalo Road (tel: 6293 3664). No credit cards.

Singapore Zam Zam Restaurant $ *697–699 North Bridge Rd; tel: 6298 6320.* Open daily. A rough-and-ready place serving Indian-Muslim specialities. The fragrant mutton or chicken *biryani* (with saffron rice) is robustly spicy, as are the flaky breads, called *murtabak* when stuffed with minced mutton or chicken, and *prata* when eaten plain and dipped in curry.

ORCHARD ROAD

Basilico $$$$ *Level 2, Regent Hotel, 1 Cuscaden Road; tel: 6725 3232.* www.regenthotels.com. Open daily breakfast, lunch and dinner. This restaurant by the pool offers alfresco and indoor dining. Aside from the a la carte menu, the outstanding antipasti buffet offers fresh seafood, salads, prosciutto ham with melon, squid ink bread and other Italian-inspired creations. The dessert selection including Italian cakes, tarts and *gelatos* is heavenly.

Chatterbox $$ *Level 5, Mandarin Orchard Singapore, 333 Orchard Road; tel: 6831 6291/88;* www.chatterbox.com.sg. Open daily for breakfast, lunch and dinner and supper. The iconic coffee house is most famous for its chicken rice which, although expensive, is worth trying. The other local specialities offered such as *nasi lemak* (coconut rice with condiments) and lobster *laksa* are just as good.

Crossroads Café $$$ *Marriott Hotel, 320 Orchard Road; tel: 6831 4605;* www.singaporemarriott.com. Open daily for breakfast, lunch and dinner. Perch yourself at this sidewalk café and watch all of Orchard Road pass by while you sample its varied and delicious mix of Singapore favourites and Asian and Western dishes.

Din Tai Fung $$ *290 Orchard Rd. B1-03 Paragon; tel: 6836 8336;* www.dintaifung.com.sg. Open daily. This wildly popular restaurant is always crowded during meal times and queuing may be necessary but it's worth the wait. The open kitchen allows diners to watch the chefs in action. Feast on the famous *xiao long bao* (steamed pork dumplings that have exactly 18 pleats each) and other equally delicious dishes such as the fried rice and chicken soup.

Hua Ting $$$ *2/F, Orchard Hotel, 442 Orchard Rd; tel: 6739 6666;* www.millenniumhotels.com.sg. Open daily for lunch and dinner. This stalwart serves traditional and innovative Cantonese delicacies created by well-known master chef Chan Kwok. Popular items include baked silver codfish with honey and dim sum.

Iggy's $$$$ *The Hilton Hotel, 581 Orchard Road; tel: 6732 2234;* www.iggys.com.sg. Open for lunch Monday to Friday and dinner Monday to Saturday. One of the restaurants ranked under the S. Pellegrino World's 50 Best Restaurants list, Iggy's is a modern European restaurant helmed by local culinary star Ignatius Chan. Savour degustation menus of inventive dishes crafted from the freshest ingredients such as *cappellini* in scampi oil.

The Line $$$$ *Shangri-La Hotel, 22 Orange Grove Road; tel: 6213 4275;* www.shangri-la.com. Open daily. This all-day buffet restaurant is one of the most popular in town, thanks to its huge variety of cuisines. The 16 culinary stations turn out freshly prepared international fare, from sushi and *dim sum to tandoori.*

Newton Food Center $ *Bukit Timah Rd (near Newton MRT).* Open daily for lunch, dinner, supper. Best visited at night when it's cooler. Ignore the touts, but make sure you choose somewhere where prices are posted prominently. Good bets include barbecued seafood and grilled chicken wings.

Straits Kitchen $$$$ *Lobby Level, Grand Hyatt Singapore, 10 Scotts Road; tel: 6732 1234;* www.singapore.grand.hyatt restaurants.com. Open daily for breakfast, lunch and dinner. All of Singapore's favourite hawker foods are gathered at this stunning upscale restaurant. Only buffet-style meals available, enabling you to take your pick from the Indian, Chinese and Malay cuisine on offer. Recommended are the fried *kway teow* and satay.

Taste Paradise $$$ *2 Orchard Turn, 04-07 ION Orchard; tel: 6509 9660;* www.paradisegroup.com.sg. Open daily for lunch and dinner. A great place for a pit-stop after all the shopping. The Cantonese menu is excellent; try the delicious dim sum items including the XO carrot cake and custard buns.

The Tandoor $$$ *Basement One, Holiday Inn Park View, 11 Cavenagh Road; tel: 6730 0153.* Open daily for lunch and dinner. One of the city's most highly rated Kashmiri restaurants, The Tandoor is best known for its fresh breads and oven-baked dishes such as the lobster tandoori.

SOUTH SINGAPORE

Osia $$$$ *Resorts World Sentosa, Crockfords Tower, Level 2; tel: 6577 6688;* www.rwsentosa.com. Open Thursday to Tuesday for lunch and dinner. Australian celebrity chef Scott Webster creates a menu inspired by fresh Aussie produce and Asian influences. Signatures include the innovative 'Seafood Ice Experience', milk-fed lamb short loin, and Valrhona hot chocolate soup.

Saint Pierre $$$$ *01-15 Quayside Isle, 31 Ocean Way. Tel: 6438-0887.* www.saintpierre.com.sg. Open for dinner Tuesday to Sunday, lunch Saturday and Sunday. This well established modern French restaurant owned by celebrity chef Emmanuel Stroobant impresses with his sophisticated seasonal menu. Signatures include Stroobant's foie gras creations, oven-baked black cod with white miso and flourless chocolate cake.

Skirt $$$$ *W Singapore – Sentosa Cove, 21 Ocean Way; tel: 6808-7278;* www.wsingaporesentosacove.com. Open Tuesday to Sunday for dinner. A vibrant dining experience awaits meat lovers at Skirt. Beef is aged in glass cabinets and chefs fire up all cuts of meats in the open kitchen right in the centre of the restaurant.

Tung Lok Signatures $$$ *1 Harbour Front Walk, Vivocity 01-57; tel: 6376 9555;* www.tungloksignatures.com. Open daily for lunch and dinner. This modern Chinese restaurant by the famous Tung Lok Group overlooks the water and Sentosa Island. Tuck into delicious specialities such as deep-fried prawns with wasabi-mayo sauce and rack of lamb with homemade sauce.

HOLLAND VILLAGE AND AROUND

Da Paolo Pizza Bar $$$ *Block 44 Jalan Merah Saga, 01-46; tel: 6479 6059;* www.dapaolo.com.sg. Open daily for lunch and dinner, and breakfast on Saturday and Sunday. Located on a leafy street, this well-known pizzeria with its take-it-easy vibe is ideal for a relaxing meal. The kitchen rolls out made-to-order pizzas and other delicious Italian-style dishes, as well as a weekend breakfast menu.

Min Jiang One North $$$$ *5 Rochester Park; tel: 6774 0122.* Open daily lunch and dinner. This high-end Chinese restaurant is located in a conserved black-and-white colonial bungalow in Rochester Park. The repertoire extends beyond Sichuan fare, with dishes from various Chinese regions, but the highlight is the Peking duck with eight different condiments.

Original Sin $$$$ *Block 43 Jalan Merah Saga, 01-62 Chip Bee Gardens, Holland Village; tel: 6475 5605;* www.originalsin.com.sg. Open daily for lunch and dinner. This vegetarian restaurant specialises in Italian and Mediterranean fare, with knockout mockmeat cannelloni and pizzas as well as superb risotto, pasta and salads, in a European setting.

EAST COAST

East Coast Lagoon Food Village $ *1220 East Coast Parkway, next to car park E2.* Open daily. Feast on the best local food within a stone's throw of the sea. Make a beeline for the barbecue chicken wings, satay, vermicelli with satay sauce and barbecue pork noodles. Best visited at night when all the stalls are open.

Peramakan $$ *01-02/03 Santa Grand Hotel East Coast, 171 East Coast Road; tel: 6346 4202;* www.peramakan.com. Open Tuesdays to Sundays for lunch and dinner. Authentic, boldly flavour Nonya food is served here. Specialities include beef *rendang, ayam buah keluak* (chicken braised with Indonesian *keluak* nuts) and home-made icy *chendol* dessert.

Red House Seafood $$ *Block 1204, 01-05, East Coast Seafood Centre, East Coast Parkway; tel: 6442 3112;* www.redhouseseafood. com. Open daily for lunch and dinner. There are several good seafood restaurants at the East Coast Seafood Centre along the East Coast Parkway. Red House is one of the best, offering informal outdoor dining. Dishes like chilli crab and prawns with creamy custard sauce are always fresh and superbly prepared.

A–Z TRAVEL TIPS

A Summary of Practical Information

A

ACCOMMODATION

There are hotels for every budget in Singapore. Major American and international hotel chains are well represented. Most hotels are concentrated in the Civic District (Raffles City, Marina Square areas), on or near Orchard Road and in Chinatown. The **Singapore Hotel Association**'s website (www.stayinsingapore.com) offers online hotel reservations. If you arrive without hotel reservations, the Singapore Hotel Association counters at Changi Airport can arrange bookings. Hostels and bed and breakfast accommodation are few, but there are lots of budget hotels (many with air-conditioning). Travel agents, package travel services and travel websites offer accommodation deals with substantial savings. If you're staying for a longer period, try a service apartment (www.servicedapartments.org.sg), most of which come with all the amenities of a 4- to 5-star hotel, with the added facilities of a fully equipped kitchen and dining area, for lower rates than a hotel room.

Traditionally, high season is June to July and November to January, during the school holidays and year-end festivities. Low season is February to May, August to October. Hotels offer discounted rates during that time. However, hotels are usually packed with locals who check in for 'staycations' on National Day (9 August). In September, sports fans throng the city during Formula 1 season so it's best to book at least several months ahead of time, or check out the various Formula 1 travel packages on offer.

AIRPORT

Singapore Changi Airport (tel: 6595 6868; www.changiairport.com) is frequently rated the best in the world. Disembarking passengers will discover why, as the march (assisted by travelators) through customs, immigration and baggage claim usually takes just a matter of minutes. There are three large terminals (with a fourth slated for completion in 2017). Excellent modern facilities include banks, business centres, internet access, nurseries, clinics, pharmacies and convenience stores. Taxis, shuttle vans (Maxicabs) and city buses are available at terminal entrances. A taxi ride downtown (a 16km/10-mile journey) costs about S$18–38, excluding surcharges (Fri–Sun 5pm–midnight S$5; S$3 all other times; additional surcharge of 50 percent of final metered fare daily midnight–6am). Limousine taxis cost $55 and seven-seater taxis cost $60. Taxi rides from the airport to downtown take about 20 to 30 minutes. The MRT link from the airport to City Hall station downtown takes about half an hour and costs S$1.90.

Arrive two hours early for departing flights. Leaving Singapore, all passengers must pay an airport departure tax (S$21), which is usually incorporated into your air ticket. Transit passengers waiting a minimum of five hours may qualify for free city tours organised by Changi Airport and Singapore Airlines (check at the Free Singapore Tours (FST) Registration Booth located in Terminal 2 and 3). A transit hotel is available in the three terminals, renting rooms inexpensively in six-hour increments (tel: 6507 9797; www.harilelahospitality.com). Showers, saunas and gym facilities are also available for hire for travellers wishing to freshen up during a stopover. The airport and most facilities are open daily 7am–11pm. The flight information hotline (toll-free in Singapore only) is tel: 1800-542 4422 or 65-6542 4422 (overseas).

B

BUDGETING FOR YOUR TRIP

Singapore has the second-highest standard of living in Asia (behind Japan), so expect many prices to be only slightly below those in North America and northern Europe. Flights from London to Singapore cost about £800, from the US about US$1700, and from Australia about AU$800. Food and transportation can be bargains. Meals at hawker centres and food courts can be as little as S$3. A three-course dinner in a mid-range restaurant can cost about S$50–70. Subway (MRT) fares are between S$1.10 and S$2.30. City buses are just as cheap

(S$0.90–2.90), and taxi trips around town are often as little as S$10. Hotels run the gamut, from under S$70 per room for budget choices to about S$150 for a mid-range double room, to over S$500 for top accommodation. Private city tours are priced at S$28–100 and up.

Entrance fees to sights are reasonable (S$2–18), but entertainment costs (for performances, nightclubs) can be as high as in Western capitals. Alcohol is expensive, around S$12 for a pint of beer and $14 for a glass of house wine. Many bars have a 'happy hour', usually between 5pm and 9pm, with deals such as half-price drinks.

Budget travellers can certainly visit Singapore cheaply, although other nearby Southeast Asian destinations offer much lower prices. Singapore offers convenience, cleanliness, efficiency, superb meals and some great attractions, but it is not the bargain basement of Asia.

C

CAR HIRE

Car hire is seldom necessary in Singapore since it is compact and served by excellent and inexpensive forms of public transportation, but major car rental companies operate all over the island, including at the airport and downtown in the hotel districts. The Singapore government, in a concerted effort to reduce traffic congestion, has made car rental and use, especially in the central business district, an expensive and sometimes complicated affair. Rates are about S$175 for a 1.3-litre car to S$295 for a 2-litre car per day including mileage but not insurance. Rental cars can be taken into Malaysia, but surcharges and petrol restrictions apply (the tank must be at least three quarters full upon leaving Singapore). A valid driver's licence from your country of residence or a valid International Driving Licence is required, as is a major credit card. Some companies rent cars only to those over 21 and under 60. Petrol prices are higher in Singapore than in some European countries, and up to three times higher than in the US.

Major car rental companies in Singapore include:

Avis tel: 6737 1668; www.avis.com.sg
Budget tel: 6532 4442; www.budget.com.sg
Hertz tel: 1800-734 4646; www.hertz.com
Popular 501 Guillemard Road; tel: 6742 8888; www.popularcar.com
Unique 02-574, 1 Rochor Centre; tel: 6292 7656; http://uniquecar
rental.com.sg

Avis, Budget and Hertz are the only car rental companies at Singapore Changi Airport. The counters operate from 7am to 11pm.

Hotels can often arrange for a car and driver; chauffeur-driven luxury cars can cost S$50 per hour and up.

CLIMATE

Singapore's tropical climate is fairly uniform, as are the hours of sunrise and sunset (6.30–7am/6.30–7pm), due to its location just 136 km (85 miles) north of the equator. Rainfall is heaviest from November through January. Humidity is routinely very high all year round, averaging 80–85 percent. Daytime temperatures can soar near the average maximum of 31°C (88°F) in the afternoon and nighttime lows can dip to near the average minimum of 24°C (75°F) just before sunrise. The lowest temperature ever recorded in Singapore was 19.4°C (66.9°F). Annual rainfall averages 2357.8mm (93 inches), with sudden but brief downpours common. For the weather forecast dial 6542 7788. Monthly average temperatures are as follows:

	J	F	M	A	M	J	J	A	S	O	N	D
°C	26	27	27	27	28	28	27	27	27	27	26	26
°F	79	81	81	81	82	82	81	81	81	81	79	79

CLOTHING

The island's dress code is casual but neat. Short-sleeved cotton sportswear is acceptable almost everywhere. Even businesspeople seldom wear suits or jackets. Some tourists wear shorts, as do many

Singapore residents. Mosques require that arms and legs be fully covered (by long-sleeved shirts, trousers and long skirts or sarongs) to enter. Sikh temples require visitors to wear a head covering, as do synagogues for males. Raincoats are hardly necessary, although a light sweater or wrap is sometimes required in the evening and in air-conditioned buildings and vehicles. Umbrellas are handy in a downpour. Hats, sunscreen and sunglasses are essential against the harsh tropical sun, while comfortable walking shoes or sandals are useful for long periods of sight-seeing and shopping.

CRIME AND SAFETY

Singapore has the lowest crime rate in Southeast Asia, but pickpockets and purse snatchers do operate, usually around neighbourhood markets, even though the penalty for pickpocketing is three years in jail and four strokes of the cane. Crime is also very low in hotels, which have discreet security forces, but do use the hotel safety box or room safe for valuables. Report stolen property and other crimes to your hotel and the police (tel: 999 or 1800-225 0000).

Singapore has strict laws covering infractions that might be considered minor elsewhere. Littering can result in a S$300 fine for first-time offenders. Smoking is banned in public places, including restaurants, buses and taxis; the fine is up to S$1,000. The chewing of gum is not banned, but the unauthorised sale of chewing gum is subject to a fine up to S$2,000.

Drug offences are dealt with harshly. The death penalty is mandatory for those convicted of trafficking, manufacturing, importing or exporting certain amount of drugs.

D

DRIVING

Motorists drive on the left, overtake on the right and yield to pedestrians at designated crossing points. A valid driver's licence or an International Driving Licence is required. Speed limits are 50–60 km/h (30–37 mph) in residential areas, 70–90 km/h (40–50 mph) on expressways. Singapore roads are in excellent condition and signposted in English. Speed cameras are installed throughout the island. Bus lanes or lanes with unbroken yellow lines are used only by buses during rush hours (Mon–Fri 7.30–9.30am and 5–8pm). Full-day bus lanes (Mon–Sat 7.30am–8pm) are marked by red lines

All vehicles entering the Central Business District (CBD) from 7.30am to 8pm from Monday to Saturday are required to pay an Electronic Road Pricing (ERP) toll. ERP tolls are also levied on expressways during peak hours (check details with the **Land Transport Authority**, tel: 1800-225 5582; www.lta.gov.sg). All vehicles are installed with an In-Vehicle Unit (IU) and a cash card (stored-value card). The toll is automatically deducted from the cash card each time the vehicle passes through an erp gantry. The toll varies with the time of day and entry point. The ERP is not in operation on Sunday and public holidays.

Driving information is available from the **Automobile Association of Singapore** (AAS; tel: 6333 8811; www.aas.com.sg) and the Land Transport Authority. The aas emergency road service operates 24 hours a day (tel: 6748 9911). The traffic police can be contacted at tel: 1800-547 1818.

At public car parks and for on-street parking, a pre-paid parking coupon must be displayed. These are sold at petrol stations, post offices and convenience stores. In the car parks of most shopping centres and public buildings, cash card payment is used. Depending on the system installed, you will need to insert your cash card either into a machine at the entrance or into your car's IU so the fee can be deducted when you pass through the gantry.

E

ELECTRICITY

Singapore's voltage is 220–240 A.C., 50 Hertz. Most hotels provide a transformer to convert to 110–120 A.C., 60 Hertz. Outlets require plugs with two round prongs or the three-pronged square type.

EMBASSIES AND HIGH COMMISSIONS

Open Monday–Friday, 9am–5pm, although some work shorter hours.

Australia: High Commission, 25 Napier Road, tel: 6836 4100; www.singapore.embassy.gov.au

Canada: High Commission, 11-01, One George Street, tel: 6854 5900; www.singapore.gc.ca

New Zealand: High Commission, 21-04, One George Street; tel: 6235 9966; www.nzembassy.com/singapore

South Africa: Embassy, 15-01/06 Odeon Towers, 331 North Bridge Road, tel: 6339 3319; www.dirco.gov.za

UK: High Commission, 100 Tanglin Road, tel: 6424 4200; www.uk insingapore.fco.gov.uk

US: Embassy, 27 Napier Road, tel: 6476 9100; http://singapore.us embassy.gov

EMERGENCIES

If you are in a hotel, call the front desk, operator or hotel security. General emergency telephone numbers are:

Police **999**

Ambulance/Fire **995**

24-hour Touristline **1800-736 2000**

G

GAY AND LESBIAN TRAVELLERS

Homosexual activity is illegal in Singapore. This said, there is a discreet homosexual scene and a few gay-friendly entertainment venues, mainly in Tanjong Pagar and the Chinatown area.

GETTING THERE

By air. Singapore is served by about 100 international airlines, operating about 6,400 flights a week from 250 cities. As a major Asian hub, Singapore Changi Airport is a superb stopover, frequently voted one of the world's best airports. Tickets during the high season (June to September and December to January, from Europe and North America; December to January from Australia and New Zealand) are the most expensive.

Singapore Airlines, the national air carrier, is frequently rated the world's best airline. It offers non-stop and one-stop flights to and from many cities, including Vancouver in Canada; Los Angeles, San Francisco, New York and Chicago in the US; Adelaide, Brisbane, Melbourne, Perth and Sydney in Australia; Auckland and Christchurch in New Zealand; London and Manchester in the UK; and Durban and Johannesburg in South Africa. Singapore Airlines has offices in all the countries it serves, including the United States (tel: 800-742 3333), the United Kingdom (tel: 0844-800 2380), Canada (tel: 800-663 3046), Ireland (tel: 01-671 0722), Australia (tel: 13 10 11), New Zealand (tel: 0800 808 909), South Africa (tel: 21-674 0601) and in Singapore itself (2 Orchard Turn, 04-05 ION Orchard; tel: 6223 8888; www.singaporeair.com.sg).

Singapore is also home to budget airlines Tiger Airways (tel: 6808 4437; www.tigerairways.com) and Jetstar Asia (tel: 800 616 1977; www.jetstar.com/sg).

By rail. Visitors can enter and leave Singapore via bus or rail through Malaysia. Trains operated by **Keretapi Tanah Melayu Berhad (KTMB)** (www.ktmb.com.my), connect Singapore to Kuala Lumpur and other Malaysian cities. A daily International Express Train connects Singapore to Thailand, as does the **Eastern & Orient Express** (tel: 6395 0678 in Singapore, 800-524 2420 in US; www.easternandorientalexpress.com). The Tanjong Pagar Railway Station has moved to the Woodlands Train Checkpoint (tel: 6767 5963), near the Malaysian border.

GUIDES AND TOURS

Various private and group tours are offered by Singapore tour companies. These can be booked directly or through hotel tour desks. Use guides licensed and trained by the Singapore Tourism Board (STB). Leading tour operators include the award-winning **Holiday Tours** (tel: 6734 1818/6238 2766; www.holidaytours-sin.com) and **RMG Tours** (tel: 6220 8722/6220 1661; www.rmgtours.com). The zany **DUCKTours** (tel: 6338 6877; www.ducktours.com.sg) take you from land to river as they cover key tourist sights in their amphibious half-boat, half-truck vehicles. The same company also offers city sightseeing trips on open-top double-decker bus. Visitors can hop on and off at designated stops along the way. Journeys (tel: 6325 1631; www.journeys.com.sg) offer the **Original Singapore Walks**, which take you to the more unusual places of interest, including 'wet' markets, red-light districts and war museums. If it's private taxi tours you prefer, qualified **taxi-cum-tourist guides** are available: call Singapore Taxi Academy (tel: 9025 8000; www.singaporetaxitour.com).

HEALTH AND MEDICAL CARE

Singapore has no free medical care and medical evacuation is very expensive, so be sure you are covered by your travel insurance. Most hotels have doctors on call around the clock. Singapore's medical facilities are the finest in Asia. The **Raffles Medical Clinic** (585 North Bridge Road, tel: 6311 1111; www.rafflesmedical.com) is a 24-hour clinic as is the **Singapore General Hospital** on Outram Road (tel: 6222 3322; www.sgh.com.sg). For ambulance service, dial 995. Pharmacies are open 9am–6pm, sometimes later, but it is wise to travel with your own prescriptions and medications. Drink plenty of liquids to avoid heat exhaustion and use sunscreen.

Tap water and ice are perfectly safe to consume in Singapore, but bottled water is widely available.

HOLIDAYS

The following are national holidays. Banks and government offices are closed on these dates, as are some shops. When a public holiday falls on a Sunday, the following Monday is usually a national holiday.

New Year's Day 1 January

Chinese New Year The first two days of the first lunar month; usually in January or February.

Hari Raya Haji Muslim pilgrimage celebrations; date changes annually.

Good Friday Usually in March or April.

Labour Day 1 May

Vesak Day Buddha's birthday; 8th day of the 4th lunar month, usually in May or June.

National Day 9 August

Deepavali Hindu festival; usually in October/November

Hari Raya Puasa Last day of Ramadan, 9th month of the Islamic calendar; date changes annually.

Christmas 25 December

L

LANGUAGE

Singapore has four official languages: English (the language of administration), Chinese (Mandarin), Tamil and Malay. English is widely spoken. Malay, designated as the national language, is spoken by only 15 percent of the population but understood by many Singaporeans. English serves as the island's lingua franca, although the government is attempting to discourage the use of a widespread local form of pidgin known as Singlish, or Singaporean English.

M

MAPS

Free city maps are available at Changi Airport's arrival hall, most hotels and at Singapore Tourism Board's visitor centres (see page 131). The free monthly *The Official Guide & Map* and *Where Singapore* magazine also contain maps.

Most bookshops also stock maps of Singapore. A good one to get is the **Insight Fleximap Singapore**, laminated for durability and easy folding.

MEDIA

Of the nine major daily newspapers published in Singapore, four are in English, led by *The Straits Times*, which covers local, regional and international news. *The Edge Singapore* is a business and investment weekly. Local magazines in English include *I–S*, *Time Out*, *Where Singapore* and *8 Days*, all of which cover entertainment, attractions and shopping. International newspapers and magazines are available at bookstores, newsstands, shopping centres and hotel kiosks. Some publications are subject to government-controlled circulation quotas.

Cable and satellite TV broadcasts, with CNN, BBC, MTV, NHK, ESPN and other common channels, are widely available in hotels. Local TV stations broadcast via the following channels: Channel 5 in English, Channel 8 and Channel U in Mandarin, Suria in Malay, Vasantham in Tamil. Okto shows kids' programmes, documentaries and arts content and Channel NewsAsia broadcasts news and current affairs programmes.

Eight of the local radio stations broadcast in English. Popular stations for English music include Class 95 (95FM), Gold 90FM (90.5FM) and 987FM (98.7FM). BBC World Service is also available on FM radio (88.9FM).

MONEY

Currency. The Singapore dollar (abbreviated S$ or SGD) is divided into 100 cents, with coins of 1, 5, 10, 20, 50 cents and S$1. Bills in common circulation are S$2, S$5, S$10, S$20, S$50, S$100, S$500, S$1,000 and S$10,000.

Currency exchange. Money-changing services are available at Changi Airport and at most banks, hotels and shopping centres. Licensed money changers (usually located in shopping malls) give slightly better rates than banks; hotels give the worst rates. The exchange rates at the airport are on a par with those at downtown banks.

Credit cards. Major credit cards are widely accepted by Singapore's restaurants, hotels, shops, travel agencies and taxis. Report lost or stolen credit cards to the police (tel: 1800-353 0000). In Singapore, you can call American Express (tel: 1800-299-1997), Diners Club (tel: 6416 0800), Mastercard (tel: 800-110 0113) and Visa (tel: 800-448 1250) for replacements.

Traveller's cheques. Traveller's cheques are easy to exchange for local currency and are accepted at many stores, restaurants and hotels.

ATMs. Automated teller machines are everywhere (at banks, shopping malls and many hotels). The Cirrus and plus system machines work in Singapore just as they do overseas.

O

OPENING TIMES

Museums and tourist attractions have varying hours, but many open at about 9.30am and close at 5 or 6pm; some are closed at least one day a week. Banks are usually open Monday to Friday 9.30am–3pm, Saturdays 9.30am–12.30pm (but Saturday hours can vary). Government offices operate Monday to Friday 8am–6pm; some are open on Saturday. Many restaurants are open daily 11.30am–10pm, but hawker centres keep longer hours, from dawn to midnight daily. Department stores and shopping centres are generally open daily from 10am–9pm.

P

POST OFFICES

Letters and postcards can be dropped off at hotel front desks.

Branches of the **Singapore Post** are generally open Monday to Friday 8.30am–5pm and Saturday till 1pm. The Singapore Post branch at 1 Killiney Road is open Monday to Friday 9.30am–9pm, Saturday 9.30am–4pm, Sunday 10.30am–4pm. The Changi Airport Post Office is open daily 8am–9.30pm at Terminal 2 Departure Hall, and open daily 6am–10.30pm at Terminal 2 Transit. Post boxes are white in colour with a Singapore Post logo. DHL, FedEx, TNT and UPS provide courier services as well.

PUBLIC TRANSPORT

Buses. Singapore has an efficient public bus system (www.sbstransit.com.sg or www.smrt.com.sg). Fares are between $0.77 to S$2.90 for air-conditioned buses. Buses operate daily from 6am to midnight. Ask the driver for the fare to your destination; exact change is required and the money is deposited into a box near the driver.

Alternatively, purchase the **Singapore Tourist Pass** (tel: 6496 8300; www.thesingaporetouristpass.com.sg) at selected MRT stations. Enjoy unlimited rides on buses and trains for just S$20 a day. Also available are 2-day (S$26) and 3-day (S$30) passes. To use the card, either flash or tap it on the electronic readers mounted at bus entrances and entry turnstiles of MRT stations.

If you are planning to be in Singapore for a longer period, buy an **ez-link card** (stored-value transportation card). This costs S$12 (out of which S$7 is stored value for use) if purchased from Transit Link Ticket Offices, Concession Card Replacement Centres or Passenger Service Centres. Cards bought from 7-Eleven costs S$10, with a S$5 stored value. The remaining S$5 is a non-refundable administration charge, but the convenience of using this card far outweighs the expense. Simply tap the card on the electronic reader as you board and alight the bus.

NightRider. Night buses run from 11.30pm–4.35am on Friday, Saturday and evenings of public holidays. Trips cost a flat fee of S$4.50. They provide an inexpensive way of getting around late at night. The routes pass major nightlife areas, including Boat Quay, Clarke Quay,

Marina Bay and Orchard Road. Check www.smrt.com.sg/buses/busservices/nightrider.aspx for detailed routes.

SIA Hop-On is a tourist bus service that plys the major landmarks and attractions around the city area. As its name implies, you hop on (and off) as you wish along various designated stops. One-day tickets are S$8 for Singapore Airlines and SilkAir passengers visiting Singapore and S$25 (adult)/S$15 (child) for other passengers. Check www.siahopon.com for more info or call 6338 6877.

Subway (MRT). Singapore's Mass Rapid Transit (MRT) system is very efficient and simple to use. It operates from 5.15am–12.49am daily, with trains arriving every 2 to 3 minutes from 7am to 9am and 5 to 7 minutes during off-peak times. Single trip tickets cost between S$1.10 and $2.30, in addition to a S$1 refundable deposit. Because this can prove cumbersome, it makes more sense to get the Singapore Tourist Pass or an ez-link fare card (see above) even if you're just visiting the country for a day. Rush hours should be avoided. For information: tel: 1800 336 8900; www.smrt.com.sg; Mon–Fri 7am–11pm, Sat 9am–1pm. There are five MRT lines: the East–West, North–South, Northeast, Circle and Downtown lines.

Trishaws. Trishaw Uncle (www.trishawuncle.com.sg; tel: 6337 7111) is the only licensed operator for trishaw tours in Singapore appointed by the Singapore Tourism Board. Pick up point is at the Albert Mall Trishaw Park at Queen Street.

Taxis. Singapore's 25,000 taxis are air-conditioned and comfortable. Most of the drivers are friendly and helpful, although a few can be a bit gruff. Within the CBD (including Orchard Road) taxis can only be boarded and alighted at taxi stands and alongside roads; elsewhere in Singapore, simply flag one along the road. All taxis are metered; most accept credit cards. Basic fares are S$3–3.40 (normal taxi) or S$3.90 (limousine taxi) for the first kilometre, and 22 cents for every 400 metres travelled up to 10km, or every 350 metres travelled after 10km, and every 45 seconds of waiting time.

A variety of surcharges are thrown in for midnight to 6am trips (50 percent is added to the meter fare), peak period travel, travel into restricted downtown zones, advanced booking and airport travel. Under the ERP (Electronic Road Pricing) system, additional charges apply when the taxi passes ERP gantry points during its hours of operation.

The major taxi companies are CityCab & Comfort (tel: 6552 1111), SMRT (tel: 6555 8888), Prime Taxi (tel: 6778 0808), Premier Taxi (tel: 6363 6888), Yellow-Top Taxi (tel: 6293 5545) and TransCab (tel: 6555 3333).

T

TELEPHONE

The country code for Singapore is 65. International calls to Singapore are made by dialling the international access code for the originating country, followed by Singapore's country code and the eight-digit local number. International calls from Singapore are made by dialling the international access code (001, 013 or 019) followed by the country code, area code and local number.

Most telephones in Singapore operate using phone cards (stored value cards), which can be purchased from all post offices and convenience stores like 7 Eleven, and be used for making local and overseas calls. International calling cards can be used from any phone; simply dial the calling card's access number for Singapore and follow the instructions.

Local calls made from public phones cost S$0.10 for the first 3 minutes and S$0.10 for every subsequent 3 minutes, up to a maximum of 9 minutes. No area codes are used within Singapore. Dial 100 for local call assistance and 104 for overseas call assistance.

Mobile phones. Only users of GSM mobile phones with global roaming service can connect automatically with Singapore's phone networks. If you are planning to be in Singapore for any length of time, it is more economical to buy a local SIM card from one of the three service providers: Singtel (tel: 1626 or 6738 0123), M1 (tel: 1627 or 1800-843 8383) or Starhub (tel: 1633 or 6820 1633). These cards give you a local mobile number and cost a minimum of S$20. All local mobile numbers begin with '8' or '9'.

TIME ZONES

Singapore time is GMT+8 hours year round. Although the clock is advanced one hour in summer in some countries (such as the US and UK), it stays the same in Singapore.

TIPPING

Tipping is usually not practised in Singapore. It is not allowed at Changi Airport and discouraged in many hotels and restaurants, where a 10 percent service charge is routinely added to bills on top of the Goods and Services Tax (GST) of 7 percent. Tour guides and drivers do appreciate tips (5–10 percent). Very small tips (S$1–2) can be paid to taxi drivers, porters and hotel housekeeping staff.

TOILETS

Singapore's public restrooms are reasonably clean and are regularly inspected by health department officials. Most are free, but there's sometimes a nominal charge (S$0.10–S$0.20) for their use.

TOURIST INFORMATION

The **Singapore Tourism Board** (STB) is a superb organisation, offering mountains of free and helpful literature to visitors. Their website is www.yoursingapore.com.

STB offices abroad include the following:

Australia: Level 11, awa Building, 47 York Street, Sydney nsw 2000; tel: 02-9290 2888 or 9290 2882; email: stb-syd@stb-syd.org.au

Germany: Bleichstrasse 45, 60313 Frankfurt; tel: 069-9207 700; email: info@stb-germany.de

New Zealand: Representative Office, c/o Vivaldi World Limited, 1340-C Glenbrook Road RD1, Waiuku, Auckland; tel: 800-608 506; email: stbnz@stb-syd.org.au

UK: Singapore Centre, Grand Buildings, 1–3 The Strand, London WC2N 5HR; tel: 020-7484 2710; email: stb_london@stb.gov.sg
US: Los Angeles: 5670 Wilshire Boulevard, Suite 1550 Los Angeles, CA 90036; tel: 323-677-0808; email: losangeles@stb.gov.sg
New York: 1156 Avenue of the Americas, Suite 702, New York, NY 10036; tel: 212-302 4861; email: newyork@stb.gov.sg

The Singapore Tourism Board runs a 24-hour tourist information hotline: 1800-736 2000 (toll-free in Singapore), 65-6736 2000 (from overseas); Mon–Fri 9am–6pm. Visitor centres are at the following locations:

Singapore Visitors Centre @ Orchard: Junction of Cairnhill Road and Orchard Road (daily 9.30am–10.30pm).
Singapore Visitors Centre @ ION Orchard: Level 1 Concierge (daily 10am–10pm).
Chinatown Vistor Centre @ Kreta Ayer Square: 2 Banda Street, behind Buddha Tooth Relic Temple and Museum (Mon–Fri 9am–9pm, Sat–Sun 9am–10pm).

VISAS AND ENTRY REQUIREMENTS

Citizens of Australia, New Zealand, South Africa, the United Kingdom, the Republic of Ireland, Canada and the US as well as of the Commonwealth, Western Europe and South America need only a valid passport (good for six months) to enter Singapore for a tourist or business visit lasting up to 30 days. Tourists, however, should also carry onward/return tickets to their next destination and sufficient funds for their stay in Singapore. For longer stays, apply to the **Immigration & Checkpoints Authority (ICA)** office (10 Kallang Road; www.ica.gov.sg) or call the hotline (tel: 6391 6100) upon arrival. Vaccination certificates are required only of passengers who arrive from cholera- or yellow fever-infected areas. An immigration card, supplied before arrival, must be filled out and kept with the passport for surrender upon departure.

A complete list of prohibited, restricted and dutiable goods is available from the Customs Duty Officer, Singapore Changi Airport (24-hour customs service hotline: 6355 2000; www.customs.gov.sg).

Lost or stolen passports should be reported to the police, then to ICA (tel: 6391 6100), where temporary passports are issued, and finally to your embassy.

W

WEBSITES AND INTERNET ACCESS

For more information about Singapore visit:
www.changiairport.com.sg Changi Airport
www.stayinsingapore.com Online hotel bookings
www.yoursingapore.com Singapore Tourism Board (STB)
www.gov.sg Official Singapore government site
www.makansutra.com Details the best hawker fare
www.soshiok.com Food reviews and listings
www.sistic.com.sg Tickets for performing arts and athletic events

Wireless@SG is a system that provides free wireless connection at selected hot spots around Singapore. Visitors will need a mobile device with Wi-Fi facility, and have to register with Singapore Telecommunications (tel: 1610; www.singtel.com) and M1 (tel: 6655 5633; www.m1net.com.sg). Check www.ida.gov.sg for a list of hot spots.

Y

YOUTH HOSTELS

There is some Hostelling International (HI) accommodation, namely the **Costa Sands Resorts** at Pasir Ris, Downtown East and Sentosa, and **Hangout@Mt Emily**. Check www.hisingapore.org.sg for details. Other inexpensive accommodation offers dorms and small rooms with shared baths, such as **Fort Canning Lodge YWCA** and the **YMCA** on Orchard Road (see pages 135 and 139).

Recommended Hotels

Singapore has several of the world's top-rated luxury hotels, a number of boutique hotels, and some of the cleanest budget rooms in Asia.

Posted hotel prices tend to be fairly expensive, but hefty discounts are common. Occupancy is at its highest during the high season (August and December to the end of Chinese New Year) and reservations are recommended. You can book a room yourself on the Singapore Hotel Association's website www.stayinsingapore.com, which includes full descriptions, rates, and specials for nearly every hotel and inn in Singapore.

All accommodation accept major credit cards, except where noted. Meals are normally not included, although some hotels and resorts have package specials that include buffet breakfasts.

Each entry is marked with a symbol indicating the approximate room rate charged per night for a double room with bathroom. Prices do not include the 10 percent service charge and 7 percent goods and services tax, except where noted.

$$$$	over S$ 450
$$$	S$ 300–450
$$	S$150–300
$	under S$150

SINGAPORE RIVER

Conrad Centennial $$$ *2 Temasek Boulevard, Singapore 038982; tel: 6334 8888;* http://conradhotels3.hilton.com. Adjacent to Millenia Walk and within walking distance to Suntec City and Marina Square, this hotel has large rooms, marble-clad bathrooms, a 24-hour fitness centre and an outdoor pool. 507 rooms.

The Fullerton $$$ *1 Fullerton Square, Singapore 049178; tel: 6733 8388;* www.fullertonhotel.com. Created within a 1928 colonial landmark fronting Marina Bay, this is one of Asia's top hotels, with grand facilities and acclaimed bars and restaurants. Business travellers will appreciate its proximity to the financial district. 400 rooms.

The Gallery Hotel $$ *1 Nanson Road, Singapore 238909; tel: 6849 8686;* www.galleryhotel.com.sg. With its postmodernist architecture and compact rooms and suites decorated by young artists, this is definitely a hotel for design-conscious visitors. Many rooms overlook the Singapore River. Free internet access is provided in every room. Disabled access. 222 rooms.

Grand Copthorne Waterfront $$ *392 Havelock Road, Singapore 169663; tel: 6733 0880;* www.millenniumhotels.com.sg. Located along the Singapore River and next to Zouk nightclub, the Grand Copthorne has modern rooms and a marvellous riverside ambience. Disabled access. 574 rooms.

Novotel Singapore Clarke Quay $$ *177A River Valley Road, Singapore 179031; tel: 6338 3333;* www.novotelclarkequay.com.sg. Located beside the Singapore River and near Clarke Quay MRT, the four-star Novotel Clarke Quay offers modern rooms for business travellers. Rooms have Nespresso coffee machines and contemporary pivoting workstations. 403 rooms.

Pan Pacific $$$ *7 Raffles Boulevard, Marina Square, Singapore 039595; tel: 6336 8111;* www.panpacific.com. This luxurious hotel offers spectacular harbour views, excellent dining outlets and a 35-storey-high atrium. 778 rooms.

The Ritz-Carlton, Millenia $$$$ *7 Raffles Avenue, Singapore 039799; tel: 6337 8888;* www.ritzcarlton.com. This luxury hotel at Marina Bay which sits within landscaped grounds has larger-than-average rooms and stunning bathrooms with harbour and city views. Its Sunday champagne brunches are highly popular. It has an impressive contemporary art collection containing works by Dale Chihuly and Andy Warhol. Disabled access. 608 rooms.

CIVIC DISTRICT

Fort Canning Lodge YWCA $$ *6 Fort Canning Road, Singapore 179494; tel: 6338 4222;* www.ywcafclodge.org.sg. Located on peaceful Fort Canning Hill, the YWCA has dorms and rooms, some with private baths, for single women, couples and families. A short walk to attractions and Orchard Road. 175 rooms.

Grand Park City Hall $$ *10 Coleman Street, Singapore 179809; tel: 6336 3456;* www.parkhotelgroup.com. This business hotel is located close to popular tourist sights and major shopping malls such as Raffles City. It has a spa nestled within a courtyard. Disabled access. 333 rooms.

Hangout@Mt Emily $ *10A Upper Wilkie Road, Singapore 228119; tel: 6438 5588;* www.hangouthotels.com. An inexpensive, fun and comfortable hostel that knows just what budget travellers want. This Hostelling International (HI) hostel offers 24-hour free internet access and warm and friendly service. 61 rooms with en suite bathrooms and 25 dorm beds.

InterContinental Singapore $$$ *80 Middle Road, Singapore 188966; tel: 6338 7600;* www.ihg.com. Adjoining the air-conditioned shopping mall Bugis Junction that is built over restored pre-war shophouses, this award-winning luxury tower offers shophouse-themed rooms with Peranakan artefacts. Disabled access. 403 rooms.

Raffles Hotel $$$$ *1 Beach Road, Singapore 189673; tel: 6337 1886;* www.raffleshotel.com. The Raffles is one of the legendary hotels of Asia. Opened in 1887, it was declared a National Monument a century later. Restored to an all-suites hotel, it is thoroughly plush, worthy of Singapore's highest room rates. Its Long Bar is famous as the place where the Singapore Sling cocktail was first concocted. Disabled access. 103 rooms.

Swissôtel The Stamford $$$ *2 Stamford Road, Singapore 178882; tel: 6338 8585;* www.swissotel.com. This hotel is located near the CBD and is practically part of a large shopping complex. Contains a business centre, convention centre and a huge number of restaurants and bars (including the excellent rooftop Equinox complex), plus a luxurious spa and a well-equipped fitness centre. Disabled access. 1,261 rooms.

CHINATOWN

Hotel 1929 $ *50 Keong Saik Road, Singapore 089154; tel: 6347 1929;* www.hotel1929.com. This boutique property combines a mix of old-world Singapore architecture and nouveau-chic style. No two rooms are designed the same way and many are embellished with unique furniture from the owner's private collection. 32 rooms.

New Majestic Hotel $$ *31–37 Bukit Pasoh Road, Singapore 089845; tel: 6511 4700;* www.newmajestichotel.com. This hot boutique hotel oozes style and individuality from all corners, from the custom-designed rooms done up by some of Singapore's brightest young artists to its acclaimed modern Chinese restaurant. 30 rooms.

Parkroyal on Pickering $$$ *3 Upper Pickering Street, Singapore 058289; tel: 1800 2557 795;* www.parkroyalhotels.com. This contemporary hotel houses a luxurious spa, sprawling sky gardens and a jogging track high above the street level. The rooms, decked out in natural elements, offer views of the river and city. 367 rooms.

The Scarlet $$ *33 Erskine Road, Singapore 069333; tel: 6511 3333;* www.thescarlethotel.com. Located near Chinatown and the buzzing Club Street, this decadent, boutique hotel is luxurious and dramatic, The 80 rooms consist of five suites, 39 rooms geared towards business travellers and 36 deluxe and standard rooms. It has a roof-top bar and open-air jacuzzi.

LITTLE INDIA

Albert Court Village Hotel $$ *180 Albert Street, Singapore 189971; tel: 6339 3939;* www.stayfareast.com. Boutique hotel with nostalgic interior decor and modern facilities. Houses a North Indian and Nepalese restaurant. Has 210 rooms, some with disabled access.

Moon @ 23 Dickson $ *23 Dickson Road, Singapore 209507; tel: 6827 6666; www.moon.com.sg.* This is a no-fuss boutique hotel that's trendy, compact and comfy. It's also close to Bugis MRT station, thus making it very convenient to get to any part of the city. The room rate includes complimentary breakfast, Wi-Fi, mini bar and evening cocktail. 80 rooms.

Wanderlust Hotel $$ *2 Dickson Road, Singapore 209494; tel: 6396 3322; http://wanderlusthotel.com.* The building, constructed in the 1920s, was once an old school and the concept is totally unique. Each of the four levels were designed by award-winning local design agencies, which means it's a favourite with the arty crowd. 29 rooms.

ORCHARD ROAD

Four Seasons $$$ *190 Orchard Boulevard, Singapore 248646; tel: 6734 1110; www.fourseasons.com/singapore.* Built to compete with Asia's most upscale hotels, the elegant Four Seasons has a prime location and a vast fitness and recreation centre including four tennis courts, two swimming pools and 24-hour gym. The restaurants and bar lounge are top-notch. Disabled access. 255 rooms.

Goodwood Park $$ *22 Scotts Road, Singapore 228221; tel: 6737 7411; www.goodwoodparkhotel.com.* A national landmark dating from 1900, this grand hotel in expansive gardens off Orchard Road is renowned for its romantic interiors, history, and durian desserts. 233 rooms.

Grand Hyatt $$$ *10 Scotts Road, Singapore 228211; tel: 6738 1234; www.singapore.grand.hyatt.com.* A stone's throw from Orchard Road, this top luxury hotel has turned half its rooms into large business suites for working travellers. It has outstanding dining concepts and a popular martini bar. Disabled access. 677 rooms.

Grand Park Orchard $$ *270 Orchard Road, Singapore 23 8857; tel: 6603 8888; www.parkhotelgroup.com.* If its location right in the middle of Orchard Road doesn't impress you, its stunning exterior glass facade will. The rooms are stylishly designed, echoing the decor of the rest of the hotel. Complimentary Wi-Fi, local calls and smartphone service for club lounge members. Disabled access 308 rooms.

Hilton Singapore $$$ *581 Orchard Road, Singapore 238883; tel: 6737 2233; www3.hilton.com.* The Hilton has been a favourite of business travellers for its central location. This Hilton has a fine Italian restaurant by the rooftop pool and a lobby café famous for its baked cheesecake. Disabled access. 423 rooms.

Holiday Inn Singapore Orchard City Centre $$ *11 Cavenagh Road, Singapore 229616; tel: 6733 8333; www.ihg.com.* North of Orchard Road near the Istana, this Holiday Inn has clean, modern rooms, an efficient staff and a top-rated Indian restaurant. Disabled access. 319 rooms.

Mandarin Orchard Singapore $$ *333 Orchard Road, Singapore 238867; tel: 6737 4411; www.meritushotels.com.* Serious shoppers would do well to stay here as all the major malls and boutiques are within walking distance. Its Chatterbox restaurant is noted for its Hainanese chicken rice. 1077 rooms.

Orchard Hotel $$$ *442 Orchard Road, Singapore 238879; tel: 6734 7766; www.millenniumhotels.com.sg.* The rooms are done up in a chic East-meets-West decor. One of Singapore's top Chinese restaurants, Hua Ting, is located here. 656 rooms.

The Regent $$$ *1 Cuscaden Road, Singapore 249715; tel: 6733 8888; www.regenthotels.com.* Located a few blocks south of Orchard Road in the Tanglin shopping area, the Regent is a modern luxury hotel with elegant rooms, suites with private balconies, an airy atrium and a relaxed atmosphere. Disabled access. 440 rooms.

Shangri-La $$$ *22 Orange Grove Road, Singapore 258350; tel: 6737 3644; www.shangri-la.com.* For over 30 years, Shangri-La's flagship hotel in Singapore has won many international awards, deservedly so given its high level of service, spacious rooms, excellent fine dining and a commanding location in a large garden estate near Orchard Road. Disabled access. 750 rooms.

Sheraton Towers Singapore $$ *39 Scotts Road, Singapore 228230; tel: 6737 6888; www.sheratonsingapore.com.* A short walk from Orchard Road, this restful refurbished hotel is away from the bustle, yet still easily accessible. The fine dining Li Bai restaurant serves excellent Cantonese cuisine . 420 rooms.

Singapore Marriott Hotel $$$ *320 Orchard Road, Singapore 238865; tel: 6735 5800;* www.singaporemarriott.com. Located right at the corner of Orchard and Scotts roads, this Marriott has spacious, contemporary rooms. Tangs departmental store is just next door. Disabled access. 372 rooms.

Traders Hotel Singapore $$ *1A Cuscaden Road, Singapore 249716; tel: 6738 2222;* www.shangri-la.com. Traders' rooms are both comfortable and practical. It offers complimentary local calls and Wi-Fi, a 24-hour gym and a great semi-air-conditioned restaurant serving local specialities next to the 30-metre swimming pool. Disabled access. 546 rooms.

YMCA International House $$ *1 Orchard Road, Singapore 238824; tel: 6336 6000;* www.ymcaih.com.sg. A popular budget hotel, this YMCA has dormitories and single, twin and family rooms. There is a restaurant and a rooftop swimming pool on the premises. Requires advanced booking. 111 rooms.

SENTOSA

Hard Rock Hotel Singapore $$ *8 Sentosa Gateway, Sentosa Island, Singapore 098269;* tel: 6577 8899; www.hardrockhotels.com, www. rwsentosa.com. Live it up like a rock star and get the legendary entertainment experience. Located within the Resorts World Sentosa integrated resort, you'll definitely never run out of things to do. 364 rooms divided into rooms, suites and the more lavish Hard Rock suites. Swimming pool and beach volleyball court. Disabled access.

Shangri-La's Rasa Sentosa Resort $$$ *101 Siloso Road, Sentosa, Singapore 098970; tel: 6275 0100;* www.shangri-la.com. Singapore's only beachfront hotel overlooks the South China Sea. After its S$80 million makeover, guests can now enjoy upgraded rooms and facilities including chic restaurants, a spa and a children's club. While it is not the most convenient place to stay for access to the city, it does have a free downtown shuttle service. Disabled access. 454 rooms.

INDEX

Berlitz pocket guide

Singapore

Seventh Edition 2014

Written by J.D. Brown and
Margaret Backenheimer
Updated by Amy Van
Edited by Sarah Clark
Art Editor: Shahid Mahmood
Series Editor: Tom Stainer
Production: Rebeka Davies

Photography credits: Art Science Museum
4MR; Corbis 22, 70, 79, 83; Dreamstime 6TL,
8, 26, 101; Escape Theme Park 96; Far East
Organisation 50; iStock 2TL, 2TC, 2MC, 24; Jack
Hollingsworth/Apa Publications 3MC, 48, 64,
86, 89; Javad Namazie 56; Jonathan Koh/Apa
Publications 2/3T, 7TC, 15, 32, 45, 55, 65; Killiney
4TL; KU DETA Singapore 5TC; Mary Evans 16,
18, 19; Raffles Hotel 41; Sentosa 73; Singapore
Tourist Board 1, 3TC, 3M, 4ML, 4/5M, 5MC,
6ML, 7MC, 80, 92, 99, 102; Topfoto 20; Vincent
Ng/Apa 2ML, 3M, 3M, 4ML, 4TL, 5T 6ML, 7T, 11,
12, 28, 31, 35, 37, 38, 39, 40, 42, 43, 46, 52, 54, 58,
60, 61, 62, 66, 68, 75, 76, 77, 85, 91, 95, 105

Cover picture: Corbis

Every effort has been made to provide
accurate information in this publication,
but changes are inevitable. The publisher
cannot be responsible for any resulting
loss, inconvenience or injury.

Contact us

At Berlitz we strive to keep our guides as
accurate and up to date as possible, but if you
find anything that has changed, or if you have
any suggestions on ways to improve this guide,
then we would be delighted to hear from you.

Berlitz Publishing, PO Box 7910,
London SE1 1WE, England.
email: berlitz@apaguide.co.uk
www.insightguides.com/berlitz

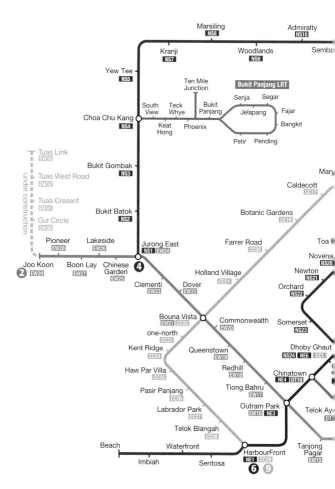

Berlitz®

speaking your language

phrase book & dictionary
phrase book & CD

Available in: Arabic, Brazilian Portuguese*, Burmese*, Cantonese Chinese, Croatian, Czech*, Danish*, Dutch, English, Filipino, Finnish*, French, German, Greek, Hebrew*, Hindi*, Hungarian*, Indonesian, Italian, Japanese, Korean, Latin American Spanish, Malay, Mandarin Chinese, Mexican Spanish, Norwegian, Polish, Portuguese, Romanian*, Russian, Spanish, Swedish, Thai, Turkish, Vietnamese
*Book only

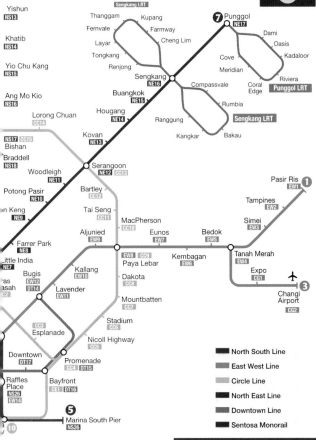

Yishun
NS13

Khatib
NS14

Yio Chu Kang
NS15

Ang Mo Kio
NS16

Lorong Chuan
CC14

NS17 CC15
Bishan

Braddell
NS18

Woodleigh
NE10

Potong Pasir
NE10

n Keng
NE9

Farrer Park
NE8

Little India
NE7

ras
asah

Bugis
EW12
DT14

Lavender
EW11

CC3
Esplanade

Downtown
DT17

Raffles
Place
NS26
EW14

a
10

Thanggam   Kupang

Fernvale   Farmway

Layar   Cheng Lim

Tongkang

Renjong

Sengkang LRT

Sengkang
NE16

Buangkok
NE15

Hougang
NE14

Kovan
NE13

Serangoon
NE12 CC13

Bartley
CC12

Tai Seng
CC11

Aljunied
EW9

Kallang
EW10

MacPherson
CC10

Compassvale

Ranggung

Kangkar   Bakau

Rumbia

Sengkang LRT

7 Punggol
NE17

Dami

Oasis

Cove   Kadaloor

Meridian

Coral   Riviera
Edge   Punggol LRT

Eunos
EW7

Paya Lebar
EW8 CC9

Dakota
CC8

Mountbatten
CC7

Stadium
CC6

Nicoll Highway
CC5

Promenade
CC4 DT15

Bayfront
CE1 DT16

5
Marina South Pier
NS26

Bedok
EW5

Kembangan
EW6

Pasir Ris 1
EW1

Tampines
EW2

Simei
EW3

Tanah Merah
EW4

Expo
CG1

✈

Changi 3
Airport
CG2

North South Line

East West Line

Circle Line

North East Line

Downtown Line

Sentosa Monorail

MRT & SBS Transit Lines